THE H2O

WORKBOOK

A Biblical Path to Hope, Heal & Overcome for the Thirsty Soul

Miriam E. Callahan, MA

The H2O Workbook

Copyright © 2017 Miriam E. Callahan

All rights reserved.

Unless otherwise indicated, all Scriptures quotations are taken from the *Holy Bible*, New Living Translation, copyright 1996, 2004, 2007, 2013 by Tyndale House Foundation. Used by permission of Tyndale House Publishers, Inc., Carol Stream, Illinois 60188. All rights reserved.

Other versions used are:

NIV—Scriptures quotations are taken from the *Holy Bible*, New International Version. Copyright 1973, 1978, 1984 by International Bible Society. Used by permission of Zondervan Publishing House. All rights reserved.

NLV—Scriptures quotation is taken from the *Holy Bible*, The New Life Version. Copyright 1969 by Christian Literature International. Used by permission of Christian Literature International. All rights reserved.

GNT—Scripture quotations are taken from the *Holy Bible*, Good News Translation. Copyright 1966, 1971, 1976, 1979 by American Bible Society. Used by permission of the Bible Societies, Harper Collins. All rights reserved.

Cover Design by Tandem Creative Designs
Interior Design by Michelle VanGeest

ISBN 978-0-692-88150-7

Printed in the U.S.A.

Table of Contents

The Ten Principles of H2O

HOPE

Principle #1: **HUMILITY**	I find hope when I humbly admit that certain areas of my life are out of control and that I am powerless to deal with life on my own terms.	*Though the Lord is great, he cares for the humble, but he keeps his distance from the proud. Psalm 138:6*
Principle #2: **TRUST**	I find hope when I reject self-sufficiency and choose a lifestyle of dependency on God.	*Trust in the Lord with all your heart; do not depend on your own understanding. Seek his will in all you do, and he will show you which path to take. Proverbs 3:5-6*
Principle #3: **SUBMISSION**	I find hope when I give control of my life and daily choices to God, recognizing that only he can heal me, change me and set me free.	*People who are ruled by their desires think only of themselves. Everyone who is ruled by the Holy Spirit thinks about spiritual things. If our minds are ruled by our desires, we will die. But if our minds are ruled by the Spirit, we will have life and peace. Romans 8:5-6*

HEAL

Principle #4: **HONESTY**	I find healing when I face the truth of my life, inviting God's Spirit to reveal what I'm unable to see on my own.	*Search me, O God, and know my heart; test me and know my anxious thoughts. Point out anything in me that offends you, and lead me along the path of everlasting life. Psalm 139:23-24*
Principle #5: **CONFESSION**	I find healing when I am willing to confess before God and another person the defects of character that he has revealed to me.	*Make this your common practice: Confess your sins to each other and pray for each other so that you can live together whole and healed. The prayer of a person living right with God is something powerful to be reckoned with. James 5:16*
Principle #6: **PERMISSION**	I find healing when I stop trying to change myself and give God permission to do whatever it takes to change me.	*Don't copy the behavior and customs of this world, but let God transform you into a new person by changing the way you think. Then you will learn to know God's will for you, which is good and pleasing and perfect. Romans 12:2*

OVERCOME

Principle #7: FORGIVENESS	I overcome by releasing resentment, bitterness and judgment toward everyone who has harmed me, yielding those areas to God alone.	*"If you forgive those who sin against you, your heavenly Father will forgive you. But if you refuse to forgive others, your Father will not forgive your sins."* Matthew 6:14-15
Principle #8: AMENDS	I overcome by taking responsibility for the harm I've caused by my words or actions, asking forgiveness whenever possible.	*Fools mock at making amends for sin, but goodwill is found among the upright.* Proverbs 14:9
Principle #9: AUTHORITY	I overcome by using the authority that Christ has given me to resist evil, refusing to tolerate darkness in my own heart.	*Submit yourselves therefore to God. Resist the devil, and he will flee from you.* James 4:7
Principle #10: SERVICE	I overcome by choosing a lifestyle that expresses God's love to a hurting world in practical ways.	*For you have been called to live in freedom, my brothers and sisters. But don't use your freedom to satisfy your sinful nature. Instead, use your freedom to serve one another in love. For the whole law can be summed up in this one command: "Love your neighbor as yourself."* Galatians 5:13-14

Guidelines for Safe Groups

1. We will safeguard the confidentiality of everyone in the group, not discussing outside of class anything another group member has revealed (even with one another).

2. Group leaders will keep all comments confidential, with these three exceptions:
   a.) If we threaten to harm ourselves
   b.) If we threaten to harm another person
   c.) If we reveal the abuse of a child

3. We will resist the temptation to advise others, focusing instead on our own healing. This includes allowing others to fully experience their emotions without interruption (such as offering them a tissue).

4. We agree to restrict our comments to 3-5 minutes in order to allow others equal time to share.

5. We will avoid the use of profanity.

THE SERENITY PRAYER
Author Unknown

God,
Grant me the serenity to accept the things
I cannot change,
the courage to change the things I can,
and the wisdom to know the difference.

Living one day at a time,
Enjoying one moment at a time,
Accepting hardship as the pathway to peace;
Taking, as Jesus did, this sinful world as it is,
not as I would have it;
Trusting that You will make all things right
if I surrender to Your will;
So that I may be reasonably happy in this life and
supremely happy with You forever in the next.
Amen.

Introduction

I remember how impressed I was the first time I heard about Mac. Mac was an older man in our church who had memorized an entire book of the New Testament. I was told that Mac could begin reciting at any point in any chapter on command. Before long I ran into Mac in the hallway. With very little prompting he was happy to quote several verses for me. I was impressed! I put him in a kind of spiritual 'Hall of Fame' in my mind. But all that changed when I got to know Mac better. Mac, the public scripture-quoter, turned out privately to be one of the most mean-spirited and angry people I'd ever met. That was when it occurred to me that information is not the same as transformation!

Information is not the same as transformation

Jesus was full of compassion for broken-hearted sinners but had little patience for those who were full of information but had very little evidence of transformation. You may know someone who has followed Christ for years, maybe even someone with lots of Bible knowledge, who like Mac has obvious character defects. If we're honest, which of us doesn't struggle with one or more habits or hang-ups we wish we could leave behind?

Most sincere Christ-followers find themselves in this predicament—they *want* to change but keep falling back into the same old habits. Why? Why is it that some people grow at an exponential rate while others get stuck in a frustrating cycle of failed attempts to change themselves?

King David of Israel knew what it was like to struggle with the condition of his soul. Listen to his words:

> *Search me, O God, and know my heart; test me and know my anxious thoughts. Point out anything in me that offends you, and lead me along the path of everlasting life.*
> Psalm 139:23-24

These words sound like they come from someone who has failed or made a mess of life. But instead they come from a man any of us would consider a great success—a powerful, wealthy and renowned king. King David could have 'rested on his laurels.' His life had been marked by prosperity and blessing. Every outward need had been met. What more could he want? But David was honest enough to humble himself—to admit that he needed God's help to truly understand the good and bad of his own heart. David had learned that being rich, successful or famous was *not* the answer. He'd learned that somewhere deep inside he lacked the ability to get life right on his own—*that being human means being flawed.*

Tragic Flaws

And so it is with you and me. First, we are born into an imperfect world. We've all been exposed to the symptoms of its imperfection. Growing up, we've experienced various levels of disappointment, pain, and rejection.

Then add to that a deep level of personal brokenness the Bible calls our *sin nature*. We deny our flaws. Some of us have perfected the art of looking good on the outside. But deep inside we can relate to the Apostle Paul's confession:

*And I know that nothing good lives in me, that is, in my sinful
nature. I want to do what is right, but I can't. I want to do what
is good, but I don't. I don't want to do what is wrong, but I do it
anyway. But if I do what I don't want to do, I am not really the
one doing wrong; it is sin living in me that does it.*
Romans 7:18-20

Because we are flawed, we all have the same three choices: we can continue to HURT, we can HIDE, or we can decide to face the truth and begin to HEAL.

Maybe you've spent a good part of your life hurting. Hurt people may struggle with anger or depression or anxiety. They try to control their circumstances in a desperate effort to make things better. Or maybe you're an expert at hiding. You look great on the outside—education, career, status. You are driven to perform well. But deep inside you worry people will discover the imperfections that lie just beneath the surface. Had enough of hurting or hiding? Why not give healing a try?

If you're willing (even if you're a bit scared), your next question might be: "What is this process all about and what can I expect from it?"

Scripture tells the new believer to "be transformed by the renewing of your mind" (Romans 12:2). Our problem isn't that we don't *want* to be transformed. It's that we don't know *how*. The H2O process is designed to take you step by step to every part of your soul (mind, emotions and will) that needs attention. It can be compared to a set of train tracks. Once you're on the right train, you know you'll end up where you need to go.

Take a look at The Ten Principles of H2O on the page just before this chapter. These tried and true biblical principles have been laid out for you. Since one builds upon the other, doing them in order will bring about the best results. Many people before you have found deep healing and freedom as they submitted to this process. You can trust the Maker of your heart to gently do the surgery you need on it!

HOPE

The first three principles of the process center on hope—hope that life can be different. So what exactly is the source of our hope? If it's found in following Christ, why is it that many Christians seem to have as many or more character flaws as non-believers? And just how much of this process is up to God and how much is up to us?

Perhaps we can find some answers in the story of the resurrection of Jesus' friend Lazarus. Let's pick up the story as Jesus approaches Lazarus' grave four days after his friend's death…

*Jesus was still terribly upset. So he went to the tomb, which was
a cave with a stone rolled against the entrance. Then he told the
people to roll the stone away. But Martha said, "Lord, you know
that Lazarus has been dead four days, and there will be a bad
smell." Jesus replied, "Didn't I tell you that if you had faith, you
would see the glory of God?" After the stone had been rolled aside,
Jesus looked up toward heaven and prayed, "Father, I thank you for
answering my prayer. I know that you always answer my prayers.
But I said this, so that the people here would believe that you sent*

me." When Jesus had finished praying, he shouted, "Lazarus, come out!" The man who had been dead came out. His hands and feet were wrapped with strips of burial cloth, and a cloth covered his face. Jesus then told the people, "Untie him and let him go."
John 11:38-44

Lazarus' Three Problems

Without a closer look, it's easy to concentrate only on the central focus of this story—Jesus has overruled nature and brought his friend Lazarus back to life after four long days of decay! This part is so amazing that it's possible to miss two lesser, but very important, details. Let's look at all three of Lazarus' problems:

Problem 1: Lazarus was dead

Without the intervention of the Son of God, Lazarus was doomed to the grave. There was absolutely nothing he could do to help himself. There was nothing his friends could do to help him. He was past hope. But Jesus showed up and everything changed. Jesus shouted the command: "Lazarus, come out!" and Lazarus came back to life! This was undoubtedly the most amazing miracle anyone there had ever seen. Lazarus knew it. Mary, Martha and their friends knew it! The whole community would be celebrating this incredible miracle that night. But before the party could begin, Lazarus still had two serious problems that Jesus personally did nothing about…

Problem 2: Lazarus was bound

Lazarus was wrapped hand and foot, even blinded by a cloth covering his eyes. When Lazarus came out of the grave, he came *out blind and hopping!* Jesus alone had the power to raise Lazarus from the dead and that's just what he did. But Jesus stopped there. He did NOT take care of Lazarus' other two problems. Instead Jesus gave the command to the friends standing nearby, "Untie him and let him go." His friends gladly did for Lazarus what he was unable to do for himself. Imagine the joy with which Lazarus' friends and family obeyed this command! Still in amazement over the miracle of his new life, they quickly set to work unwinding the strips of burial cloth. There had to be lots of advice coming from those watching: "His face—unwrap his face so he can breathe!", "Don't forget his feet—he's going to trip!" And in minutes, Lazarus is free. He's alive and he is free but he still has one really big problem….

Problem 3: Lazarus reeked

With exclamations of relief and joy, everyone begins to notice the last of Lazarus' problems—the incredible stench. His family and friends wanted to rejoice with Lazarus—to wrap their arms around him or just to get close enough to make sure he wasn't a ghost! But the putrid combination of four days of decay and the customary 70 pounds of burial spices was overwhelming, forcing his friends to give him a wide berth. Lazarus had one last problem. Yes, Jesus had raised Lazarus from the dead. Yes, his friends had loosed him. But only Lazarus could do something about the overwhelming stench. Before the celebration could begin, Lazarus needed to scrub himself clean and find some fresh clothes! Let's look now at God's solution for each of these problems.

God's Solutions

Solution 1: New Life in Christ

Like Lazarus, our biggest problem is one only God can address. At creation God warned Adam that the consequence of his disobedience would be death—physical death as well as spiritual death. We are all under that death sentence. Just like Lazarus, we each need the voice of a Savior to call us back to life. The Apostle Paul made it clear that Jesus and Jesus alone could set him free from death:

> *Oh, what a miserable person I am! Who will free me from this life*
> *that is dominated by sin and death? Thank God!*
> *The answer is in Jesus Christ our Lord.*
> Romans 7:24-25

Solution 2: The Help of Friends

Jesus could have personally loosed Lazarus from his grave clothes but didn't. He left the task to Lazarus' friends. Jesus understood the importance of relying on friends for our healing process. Today, scientists are exploring the healing power of friendship. On March 17, 2013, CBS's Sunday Morning show featured this article:

> "Friends can help you shoulder burdens, literally. At the University of Virginia, psychology professor Dennis Proffitt and a team of graduate students demonstrated how they've been asking students—either alone, or with a friend standing by—to put on a heavy backpack and estimate the steepness of a hill: on paper, by looking at a pie chart, and by using a tilting device. The overall results are unequivocal: "They find the hill to be steeper if they're alone, and less steep when they're with a friend," said Proffitt. "Moreover, if you look at the strength of their friendship, the more time they spend together with their friend, the shallower the hill appears."

Other studies have shown that people with a circle of friends tend to be healthier and to live longer. That's why the H2O process is done in the company of a small group of people that are (or will soon become) trusted friends. Although the process could be done on your own, it's not the best route to take.

There are three huge benefits to experiencing the process with friends: 1) the heaviness of the process is lightened by sharing it with others, 2) listening to others gives the Holy Spirit space to penetrate your own walls of self-protection, and 3) your life will be enriched by the depth of connection and emotional intimacy that occurs as a natural by-product of this process. Amy Carroll from Proverbs 31 Ministries says it this way:

> "I surround myself with truth-telling friends who love me deeply despite my flaws, but also have a clear view of those flaws. They're the ones who don't shrink back from telling the truth, but who stir love, kindness and gentleness into the hard things I need to hear. They celebrate my successes and mourn my defeats."

—Amy Carroll, *The Opinion Blender*, 8/6/12, Proverbs 31 Ministries

Referring to the deep level of honesty this process engenders, a group member recently made this comment: "This transparency gave me the feeling of being a *part of* the human race not *apart from* the human race!"

Solution 3: Personal Responsibility

Once Lazarus was restored to life and could walk freely, he still had some serious scrubbing to do. His body had been subjected to four days of decay mixed with layer upon layer of burial spices. He needed a bath and some fresh clothing. No one but Lazarus could deal with the personal aspect of his need. Are we any different? God gives us new life in Christ, our friends provide support and assistance along the way, but we alone are responsible for cleaning up some of our messes and for making new life choices. Our journeys may vary, but all of us need to be purified from the junk life has splashed on us! God allows us to choose. He gives us the right to say yes or no, the right to say when and if we will live our lives on his terms or on our own. Maybe it's this choice that accounts for the many Christ-followers who appear unchanged even decades after they've been given new life in Christ.

Layers

Since being human also means being flawed, we find ourselves in need of a process that will expose our flaws (the hidden ones as well as the obvious ones) and move us toward healing. This process does *not* happen automatically. Like King David, we must be intentional about giving God permission to search our hearts and show us what's hidden there.

As we do, we'll notice that most of us are unaware of the connection between the surface issues with which we struggle (issues like anger, perfectionism, worry, broken relationships, addiction and lust) and the roots of those issues (we'll be covering those very soon).

We will never become spiritually mature people, shaped into the image of Christ, without allowing Him the space and time to expose and heal the junk hidden deep in our hearts. We can do this! Together we can deal with the layers of junk in our lives in an intentional, healthy way—a way that will result in meaningful life change. Will you make the commitment?

DISCUSSION QUESTIONS:

1. What are your fears and concerns as you face the H2O process?

2. This chapter says that because we are flawed, we all have the same three choices. We can continue to HURT, we can HIDE, or we can decide to face the truth and begin to HEAL. Have you been more likely to hurt, to hide, or to heal? Describe:

3. List the problems you have struggled to overcome. (Some common areas are anger, control, resentment, bitterness, perfectionism, drivenness, depression, anxiety, and addictions of any kind—food, porn, gaming, gambling, alcohol, prescription and/or street drugs, etc.)

4. The problems we identify are often symptoms of much deeper-rooted issues such as fear, pride (an unhealthy focus on self), unhealed wounds (rejection, betrayal, ungrieved losses, abuse), unmet emotional needs (often from childhood), or the inability to view and accept God as a loving Father. What are some possible core issues that may be affecting you?

5. What areas of your life would you like to see changed as a result of this process?

1.0 Humility

Principle One: Humility

I find hope when I humbly admit that certain areas of my life are out of control and that I am powerless to deal with life on my own terms.

Though the Lord is great, he cares for the humble, but he keeps his distance from the proud.
Psalm 138:6

Sometimes the image we portray to the public is not what's really going on inside at all. Some of us have become experts at hiding the truth. Listen to Brian's story:

> By all outward appearances, my life was under control and on track. Everything was going according to my plan. My career was on fire, I had a beautiful wife, and we had a great church. I was the guy people looked at and said, "He has it all together." I made sure that was the image I portrayed. However, deep inside I was certain if people saw the real me, they would be repulsed. My sexual addiction had taken me down a very dark path. I had developed a pattern of compromising my values. I was a fraud. When my secret life was finally exposed, I had no choice but to humble myself. I surrendered my brokenness to God, to my wife, and to my pastors. I began the H2O process. Over the next two years, I shared my story with others. I stopped the protecting the secret self that kept me in bondage and I began walking down a path of honesty and openness. By humbling myself and submitting to a path of healing, God opened my eyes to a life that I'd been too afraid to seek. The transformation process was painful but I had to submit, humble myself, and trust the process in which God had placed me. Was it worth it? In every way! God has revealed and healed the core issues that fed my addiction. He has transformed the way I think and the way I live. The result: five years of freedom!

It's Universal!

Brian needed to humble himself and admit just how out of control his life had become. He had always been powerless to change himself, but he stayed stuck until he stopped lying to himself and admitted the truth. Our circumstances may be different, but if we are willing to be honest we will soon find ways that we too have been living in self-deception. We want to believe that we're okay. The 1970's even produced a very popular book entitled, *I'm Okay, You're Okay*. But God says that we're *not* okay. In fact, he says there's something broken inside all of us, something that renders us incapable of being intrinsically honest. Listen to the words of the Old Testament prophet Jeremiah:

The heart is deceitful above all things and beyond cure.
Who can understand it?
Jeremiah 17:9

This should not surprise us. Adam and Eve's decision to become masters of their own fate brought the curse of sin that has been passed down to every human born since.

When Adam sinned, sin entered the world. Adam's sin brought
death, so death spread to everyone, for everyone sinned.
Romans 5:12

How We Lie to Ourselves

Psychologists confirm what the Bible teaches about humanity's tendency to self-deceive. Defense mechanisms explain how people distance themselves from a full awareness of unpleasant thoughts, feelings and behaviors. We don't like pain so we find ways to avoid facing it. Functioning just below the surface, defense mechanisms are very effective in helping us avoid the truth. Here are three of the most common:

1. Denial

Denial is the most common of all defense mechanisms. When we use denial, we refuse to accept the reality of a fact or experience. Denial may be used by victims of trauma as a protection from overwhelming pain. People who use alcohol or drugs to cope with life tell themselves things like: "I can stop anytime I want" or "It's not like I'm addicted or anything." This also applies to compulsive eaters, shoppers, gamblers, and gamers. In the long run however, denial can prevent us from facing unpleasant information about ourselves and from finding the healing we so desperately need.

If we claim we have no sin, we are only fooling ourselves
and not living in the truth.
1 John 1:8

2. Blaming

Blaming is a convenient tool that allows me to avoid facing my own failures by focusing on yours! Blaming started as soon as sin entered the Earth: "It was the woman you gave me that made me do it!" Addicts avoid facing their own faults by blaming their problems on others (or on the system). Codependents avoid the dirt on their own doorstep by focusing on the dirtier doorstep of those close to them. And religious legalists condemn others in order to avoid facing their own faults. Jesus was pretty straightforward about the danger of this tendency:

"And why worry about a speck in your friend's eye when you have
a log in your own? How can you think of saying to your friend, 'Let
me help you get rid of that speck in your eye,' when you can't see

past the log in your own eye? Hypocrite! First get rid of the log in
your own eye; then you will see well enough to deal with the speck
in your friend's eye."
Matthew 7:3-5

3. Repression

When we use repression, we push down our unpleasant or painful thoughts and feelings. We conveniently forget them. It's the 'ostrich in the sand' method of coping—if I can't see it, it's not there. Unfortunately, repressed memories, thoughts and feelings never go away. They just lie there stagnating with time. Relief won't come until we humble ourselves and get honest:

> *Oh, what joy for those whose disobedience is forgiven, whose sin is*
> *put out of sight! Yes, what joy for those whose record the Lord has*
> *cleared of guilt, whose lives are lived in complete honesty! When I*
> *refused to confess my sin, my body wasted away, and I groaned all*
> *day long. Day and night your hand of discipline was heavy on me.*
> *My strength evaporated like water in the summer heat. Finally, I*
> *confessed all my sins to you and stopped trying to hide my guilt. I*
> *said to myself, "I will confess my rebellion to the Lord." And you*
> *forgave me! All my guilt is gone.*
> Psalm 32:1-5

Why Should We Face Our Junk?

Why should we face our painful junk? Isn't it better to let sleeping dogs lie or to just to get on with life? There is one very important reason to get this honest with ourselves—what isn't faced can't be brought to God for healing (our hurts) or for cleansing (our sins). *You can't change if you don't admit you have a problem.*

The stuff we avoid can keep us stuck for years in the same old patterns. That's what pride does. It says 'I'm fine' when nothing could be farther from the truth. Pride can prevent us from finding the healing and freedom we so desperately need. We don't want to hurt, but…

You can't change if you don't admit you have a problem

> *The Lord is close to the brokenhearted;*
> *He rescues those whose spirits are crushed.*
> Psalm 34:18

It can be scary to come clean about our sins, but…

> *People who conceal their sins will not prosper, but if they confess*
> *and turn from them, they will receive mercy.*
> Proverbs 28:13

Three Sources of Truth

We can get honest, but not without help. Real honesty comes when we take advantage of all three of these sources of truth:

1. The Holy Spirit

God is waiting for us to come to him for truth. He is willing, but won't force us to do so. God honors our intentional honesty and humility with truth and it's the truth that sets us free.

> *You rescue the humble, but you humiliate the proud.*
> Psalm 18:27

> *God makes fun of those who make fun of the truth but gives loving-favor to those who have no pride.*
> Proverbs 3:34 (NLV)

You can't trust yourself, but you can trust God. Begin the process now with this prayer from King David's words from Psalm 19:12: *"How can I know all the sins lurking in my heart? Cleanse me from these hidden faults."*

2. Trusted Friends

Those closest to us are often aware of our junk in ways we are not. Choose a person you trust to walk with you on this journey toward truth and healing. Ask them to gently share one or two areas they believe may be blind spots for you. (Most find it best to choose a friend of the same gender, not a spouse or close relative.)

> *As iron sharpens iron, so a friend sharpens a friend.*
> Proverbs 27:17

3. Our Patterns

In our life patterns, we can see the consequences of our past choices. If there is an area you see cropping up three or more times in your life, you can be pretty sure it's not a coincidence—it's a pattern. God says there's a sowing and reaping process to our choices. What we have sown in the past is evident by what we are currently reaping.

> *Do not be deceived: God cannot be mocked.*
> *A man reaps what he sows.*
> Galatians 6:7 (NIV)

Common Flaws or Problems

Check all that apply to your life in the past year:

___Anger

___Addiction (chemicals: nicotine, alcohol, drugs including prescription)

___Addiction (food)

___Addiction (sex: lust, porn affairs, romance novels, multiple serial relationships)

___Addiction (habits that consume: internet use, video gaming, gambling, shopping, work, education, church)

___Anxiety/worry

___Broken relationships

___Codependency (rescuing those we love from consequences of their own poor choices)

___Controlling others

___Depression

___Debt

___Irresponsibility

___Loneliness

___Low self-esteem

___Perfectionism

___People-pleasing

___Selfishness

___Self-harm

___Self-sabotage

___Other(s)

DISCUSSION QUESTIONS:

1. Are you more likely to deny, blame or repress uncomfortable truths about yourself or your life? Describe.

2. Share your list of known flaws with your group. What are some of the ways you have been trying to change yourself?

3. What are the issues you've been avoiding? List the here and then "own" them by admitting them out loud to your group.

4. What sources of truth are you actively pursuing?

2.0 Trust

Principle Two

**I find hope when I reject self-sufficiency and choose
a lifestyle of dependency on God.**

*Trust in the LORD with all your heart; do not depend on your own
understanding. Seek His will in all you do,
and He will show you which path to take.*
Proverbs 3:5-6

Independence—it's an American thing. Since childhood, everything we've been taught says that independence is good, that dependency equals weakness, and that strength is an important goal in life. We admire superheroes, rebels, and conquerors. Contemporary psychologist George Weinberg got it right: "As I said, men value their independency in a weird way, above practically everything."

All of this *sounds* good. But there's a problem here—God's wisdom says the opposite. A review of the scriptures reveals that man was designed with needs. Not just physical needs, but emotional and spiritual needs that can only be met in relationship with God Himself. God was so frustrated and grieved by the stubborn refusal of his people to depend on him that he sent them this message through the Old Testament prophet Jeremiah:

*"For my people have done two evil things: they have abandoned
me—the fountain of living water. And they have dug for themselves
cracked cisterns that can hold no water at all!"*
Jeremiah 2:13

God is trying to show His people just how insane it is to attempt to live life without depending on Him. Nothing has changed. You and I are hard-wired in such a way that we will never experience fulfillment outside of an intimate relationship with God. We find a reward waiting for us when we place ourselves in this distinctly dependent position:

*The LORD is good to those who depend on Him,
to those who search for Him.*
Lamentations 3:25

Jesus was perfect yet he lived a life of consistent dependency on his father. He zeroed in on the importance of this concept when some religious teachers of his day came to test him. One of them, an expert in religious law, tried to trap Him with this question: 'Teacher, which is the most important commandment in the law of Moses?' Jesus replied like this:

*"You must love the LORD your God with all your heart,
all your soul, and all your mind. This is the first and greatest
commandment. A second is equally important:
love your neighbor as yourself."*
Matthew 22:37:39

Jesus saw right through the religious leaders' façade. He knew that with all their outward goodness, they lacked healthy relationships with God the Father and with others. So it is with us. If we want to be spiritually healthy, we must begin with the right mindset.

We *Need* God

Pride is forced to take a back seat when we admit that we were created for dependency on God. We *need* God. We can deny it but we are not 'just fine' on our own. We *will* be dependent on something or someone (even if it's only ourselves). Some of us depend on our status in life, our career, our education, or our successes in order to feel okay about ourselves. Others rely on alcohol, prescription or street drugs to deal with life. We may not admit that we're using them to cope with life. We just need them for our headaches or insomnia—just a glass or two of wine to help us sleep. For some it's our appetite for food or for sex that never seems to be satisfied. Still others of us depend on other people to make us feel okay on the inside. We hang onto the relationship we have, desperately searching to find a replacement if that one should fail. And then there's the never-ending need for material things—we must have the latest and best of whatever new toy comes along.

The truth is that we *are* dependent beings. None of these 'god substitutes' can ever fill our inner void—the one God created to be filled in a loving relationship with Him.

Trusting More & Trusting Less

Living in dependency means admitting I don't have what it takes on my own. It means both trusting *less* and trusting *more*. I must trust myself less (my judgment, my strength, and my willpower) and trust God more—learning more of his true character and stretching my concept of his trustworthiness.

> "If God is the Creator and we are the creation, we have to depend on him for life and provision. Independency is not an option for us. God existed without us, not vice versa. So the role we must take in life is not only *for* dependency, but also *against* self-sufficiency."
> —Drs. Henry Cloud and John Townsend, *How People Grow*

I'll never forget the night God began to teach me this lesson. I was listening to worldwide evangelist Sammy Tippit. Sammy began his sermon that night by explaining that self-reliance is his default coping style. Like a lot of people, Sammy had the ability to impress people with his natural gifts and talents. He was doing well. But he told the crowd that night that his life was forever changed (and incredible things began to take place) when he finally understood how weak he truly was. I remember hearing him say that he begins each day with the words "I need you today, God." I made up my mind that night to begin that practice myself. For the next year, I began each day with the phrase "I need you, God." When I started the practice, I believed it only in my head. It took three months for the Holy Spirit to take this truth past my head into my heart. Like Sammy, I discovered the *secret* of weakness. God delights to show up in strength when we admit our weakness!

The Profound but 'Simple' Gospel

What does it take to restore a distant or broken relationship with God? That's what Nicodemus, a Jewish religious leader of Jesus' day needed to understand. Nicodemus was an expert in the law of Moses. He recognized that Jesus was sent from God, but he was confused when Jesus told him that no one can enter the Kingdom of God without being born of water and of the Spirit. Nicodemus knew the physical birth process involved the breaking of a sack of water, but he couldn't grasp what being 'born of the Spirit' meant. Jesus didn't want Nicodemus to miss this point so he continued to drive it home with these words:

> *No one has ever gone to heaven and returned. But the Son of Man has*
> *come down from heaven. And as Moses lifted up the bronze snake on*
> *a pole in the wilderness, so the Son of Man must be lifted up, so that*
> *everyone who believes in Him will have eternal life. For God loved the*
> *world so much that He gave His one and only Son, so that everyone who*
> *believes in Him will not perish but have eternal life. God sent His son*
> *into the world not to judge the world, but to save the world through Him.*
> *There is no judgment against anyone who believes in Him.*
> John 3:13-18

Jesus paid with His life so that our relationship with God could be restored. It didn't make sense then and it doesn't make sense now. That's because it's not about fairness—it's about grace! Grace says that God has made a way for us to enter the kingdom of heaven without doing anything to earn it. All we have to do is believe. But Nicodemus was a lot like us. Many of us grew up hearing that we somehow must earn our way to heaven or at least that our good deeds should outweigh our bad. Grace stands in complete opposition to that human thought process. The Apostle Paul wanted to ensure that the new believers in Rome understood the truth about grace:

> ***For (the people of Israel) don't understand God's way of making***
> ***people right with Himself. Refusing to accept God's way, they cling***
> ***to their own way of getting right with God by trying to keep the***
> ***law. For Christ has already accomplished the purpose for which the***
> ***law was given. As a result, all who believe in Him are made right***
> ***with God...as the scripture tells us, "anyone who trusts in Him***
> ***will never be disgraced."***
> Romans 10:3-4, 11

We will never move forward to deeper levels of intimacy with God as long as we maintain our right to decide the course of our own spiritual health. We are the created, not the Creator. We stand in need of the One who knows how we are made and what is best for us. We must admit that we *need* God! We can make a decision right now to...

STOP Depending on Ourselves and
START Depending on God!

A Prayer for Deepened Dependency on God

I need you, God. Here and now I reject my tendency to
rely on myself and choose to depend on you alone.
I believe that Jesus came to pay my sin debt and
I choose to trust you to the best of my ability.
In Jesus' name, Amen.

DISCUSSION QUESTIONS:

1. Is it a struggle for you to depend on God? How easy is it for you to slip into self-sufficiency? Describe.

2. What are some of the 'god substitutes' on which you've been dependent? Consider status, success, pleasure, possessions, and/or people.

3. Many people exhaust themselves in an effort to earn God's favor. In what ways have you done this?

4. In what areas are you rejecting self-sufficiency and living a life of dependency on God?

3.0 Submission

Principle Three

I find hope when I give control of my life and my daily choices to God, recognizing that only He can heal me, change me and set me free.

Those who are dominated by the sinful nature think about sinful things, but those who are controlled by the Holy Spirit think about things that please the Spirit. So letting your sinful nature control your mind leads to death. But letting the Spirit control your mind leads to life and peace.
Romans 8:5-6

What thoughts and feelings come into your mind when you hear the word 'submission'? For much of my early life the feelings I had were completely negative. I grew up in the 60's and was a card-carrying member of N.O.W. (the National Organization of Women). I remember thinking, "no man is *ever* going to tell me what to do!" One day I heard my Sunday School teacher say that wives must submit to their husbands. I was so mad I stood up and walked out of the class. A few months later while attending a Women's Retreat, I was chagrined to hear the teacher ask, "Ladies, would you like to hear my definition of submission?" 'No,' I thought. But the teacher continued, "submission is *ducking* so God can hit your husband!" Finally—a definition I liked! Over the years, I began to understand that every believer must learn to release control of their lives into to the hands of a loving, powerful Father.

How hard is it for *you* to submit control of your life to God? Although it may stretch you, you will never become spiritually mature until you:

1. Face your tendency to avoid the truth of your own heart,
2. Choose to live in a trusting, dependent relationship with your heavenly Father, and
3. Transfer control of your life to him.

Submitting (or giving up control) can be hard for anyone. But are there any factors that set a person up for an even stronger need to control? It's easy to see how strong-willed people might demand to be in control. But I'm convinced that even naturally passive or compliant people can struggle to a great degree with a need for control. The more chaotic a person's childhood years were, the higher their need for control. Some important factors are: growing up with an angry or addicted parent, having been the victim of abuse, and/or having been deprived of basic emotional needs. All of these situations can generate roots of fear and insecurity that are frequently expressed in control tactics.

Control Destroys

It's important to realize that although God truly *could* control the world, he chooses not to. Instead, he gives us the gift of free will even when it means allowing us to grieve him with our sinful and even evil choices.

In contrast, humans don't have the power to control anyone or anything (without force) but we keep on trying! God knows how damaging control is to the human heart and asks that we control only ourselves (our own choices, thoughts, and behaviors).

According to John Townsend, author of the best-selling book *Boundaries*, there are three things you can't change: 1) other people, 2) other people, and 3) other people!

Submission may be an unpleasant word in today's world, but it's what God asked of Jesus in his earthly life and it's what he asks of us as his children. We may not realize that relinquishing control will change our lives for the better, while living life as a controller will damage the ones we love most.

Control and Marriage

Control within marriage destroys in love feelings, but many of us seem addicted to controlling those around us. How did this all get started? The third chapter of Genesis helps us understand:

• Wives can attempt to control their husbands as part of the curse placed on Eve:

> *Then He said to the woman, "I will sharpen the pain of pregnancy,*
> *and in pain you will give birth.*
> *And you will* **desire to control** *your husband..."*
> Genesis 3:16a

• Men control due to their fear of losing their loved one or from a need to dominate their mate.

Some men who control (and even abuse) their mates have often had little or no positive fathering. Since a woman was their *only* source of emotional input, they will then attempt to draw all their emotional needs from the current woman in their lives. These men control because they are desperately afraid of losing their loved one. Other men attempt to dominate to maintain a macho image. They represent the second half of the curse placed on women:

> *"And you will desire to control your husband,*
> *but* **he will rule** *over you."*
> Genesis 3:16b

The good news is that Jesus came to redeem us from every curse of the fall. He restored women to the place of equality that God created for them in the beginning. Although the world continues to do things in its old unredeemed way, the church was created by Jesus to be a place of equality between the genders.

What are the Symptoms of a Control Problem?

- You are preoccupied over negligible details
- You experience frequent anger, especially when things don't go your way
- You are insecure
- You are critical of self and others
- You are obsessed with creating a favorable impression
- You continually try to impose your thinking on others

How strongly does the need to control affect your life? Answer the following questions as honestly as possible, maybe even thinking about how *others* see you:

The Control Test

___ It's difficult for me to trust people.
___ I make lists for everything in my life.
___ I can't stand it when I'm in a car but not driving.
___ As much as possible, I need to do everything myself.
___ I rarely think I'm wrong. (Be honest!)
___ I love to be the center of attention.
___ When it comes to social gatherings, I prefer to do the planning.
___ I get bored when I have to listen to other people talk.
___ My vacations tend to be structured and active.
___ I tend to think I know what's best for other people.
___ I don't like people touching my stuff.
___ When I'm in a relationship, I like to know where my significant other is at all times.
___ I'm definitely a perfectionist—and my own worst critic.
___ It's hard for me to get used to a new hairstyle or new pair of jeans.
___ I would not really enjoy a surprise party thrown for me.
___ I can't stand to wait for people who are running a few minutes late.
___ I am a completely stubborn person.
___ I tend to interrupt people a lot.
___ I don't like taking orders.
___ I don't take it lightly when people disagree with me.
___ Other people's messes really bother me.
___ When I'm watching TV with other people, I always have to have the remote.
___ I am easily irritated.
___ I am insulted when people don't take my advice.

Total _____

*The Control Test is taken from the book *Imperative People* by Drs. Henry Cloud and John Townsend.

Most people will check at least five to eight of these statements. If you checked nine or more statements, you are likely a candidate for unnecessary emotional stress or tension and you exhibit signs of a strong need to control.

If you believe you might be a control freak, the good news is you *can* be free! You can turn in your resignation as Official Boss of the Universe and relinquish control of your life to God. If you do, you can expect to find increased peace and hope.

For some of us control is the biggest issue that gets in the way of submission. For others of us, it's rebellion. At its core, rebellion is demanding your own way. It is refusing to bow to the will of others in authority over you. Take an honest look back over your life. How and when did you rebel against an authority figure? Rebellion is especially dangerous as it is the hallmark of the kingdom of darkness. Lucifer rebelled against God, was then cast out of heaven, and now leads his troops in rebellion against God's will and ways. (We will take a closer look at this concept in Chapter 9.0, Authority.)

Let's look at the submission principle again:

Principle Three: Submission

I find hope when I give control of my life and my daily choices to God, recognizing that only He can heal me, change me and set me free.

How Do We Relinquish Control?

Paul gave the church in Rome instructions about releasing control…

Live under the control of the Holy Spirit.
If you do, you will think about what the Spirit wants.
The way a sinful person thinks leads to death. But the mind
controlled by the Spirit brings life and peace.
Romans 8:5-6

If releasing control means living a life of submission to God, we need a clear understanding of what that looks like. The dictionary defines submission this way: 1) to yield oneself to the authority or will of another and 2) to consent to abide by the opinion or authority of another. Submission simply means *yielding control of your life to God, every day.* It's a question of who's driving the bus and it often means changing seats with God.

Everything in our world encourages the opposite. We want things our way, in our timing. God will not force us to submit to him. It's our decision. Just like the father of the prodigal son, God will allow us to go our own way even if our stubborn choices lead us toward disaster. In life, there's an easy way and there's a hard way—it's our choice! Call it stubbornness, call it selfishness or call it rebellion, we don't easily let go of control…

Do not be like the horse or the mule,
which have no understanding but must be
controlled by bit and bridle
or they will not come to you.
Psalm 32:9

The Solution

Although submission can appear like bondage, it's actually the path to an amazing life of peace and freedom. Your *willingness* probably depends on the depth of your *trust* in God. Do you trust Him until life gets scary or are you willing to give control of every single aspect of your life to him right now? If you are willing, pray this prayer now:

The Submission Prayer

Dear God,
To the best of my ability I now choose to give you complete control
of my life and my daily choices. I trust that you want only good for
me. I believe that as I submit to you, you will heal me,
change me and set me free.
In Jesus' name, Amen.

DISCUSSION QUESTIONS:

1. How did you score on the Control Test? Do you feel this score accurately represents your current attitude?

2. Rebellion is the opposite of submission. In what ways did you rebel in your early life? (Consider your relationship with your parents, teachers/coaches, police and authority figures, bosses, pastors/religious leaders.)

3. Do you see signs of rebellion against God in your current life? Describe:

4. What do you think it would take for you to make a total commitment of every area of your life to God?

5. What fears might be preventing you from taking this step?

*You can go even deeper into this principle by making a *Total Commitment* of your life to God. When you're ready, read through the Total Commitment statement, slowly considering each item. Are you willing to yield each of these areas to God?

Total Commitment

I commit:

- ✓ My Will (Decisions)
- ✓ My Mind (Thoughts)
- ✓ My Emotions (Feelings)
- ✓ My Body
- ✓ My Future (Plans, Hopes, Dreams)
- ✓ My Geographical Location
- ✓ My Home & Marriage (Family, Mate, Children)
- ✓ My Recreation & Entertainment
- ✓ My Career
- ✓ My Past Successes, Failures, & Hurts
- ✓ My Habits
- ✓ My Finances
- ✓ My Problems
- ✓ My Time
- ✓ My Integrity, Character, Attitudes
- ✓ My Business Conduct & Relationships
- ✓ My Response to Authority

I Give Up All of These Rights:

- ✓ My Right to Possessions
- ✓ My Right to a Good Reputation
- ✓ My Right to Have Acceptance
- ✓ My Right to Be Successful
- ✓ My Right to Have Pleasant Circumstances
- ✓ My Right to Presume on the Will of God
- ✓ My Right to Life Itself
- ✓ My Right to Beauty or Strength
- ✓ My Right to Have Friendships
- ✓ My Right to Be Heard
- ✓ My Right to Take on Other's Offenses
- ✓ My Right to Avoid Reaping What I Sow
- ✓ My Right to Be Right
- ✓ My Right to See Results

I give God permission to do anything He wishes to me, with me, in me, or through me that would glorify Him. I claimed these once as mine, but now they belong to God and are under His control. He can do with them anything He pleases.

Signature _____ Date _____

4.0 Honesty

Principle Four

I find healing when I face the truth of my life, inviting God's Spirit to reveal what I'm unable to see on my own.

Search me, O God, and know my heart; test me and know my anxious thoughts. Point out anything in me that offends you, and lead me along the path of everlasting life.
Psalm 139:23-24

True discipleship requires the removal or healing of all our hidden junk—every thought, attitude, or action we've chosen in rebellion to God and His ways, every wound we received, and every aching void. When we think about the good news of the gospel, we sometimes forget that Jesus died to take away more than just our sins. Listen to these prophetic words about Jesus:

*Yet it was **our weaknesses** he carried; it was **our sorrows** that weighed him down. And we thought His troubles were a punishment from God, a punishment for His own sins! But He was pierced for our **rebellion**, crushed for **our sins**. He was beaten so we could be whole. He was whipped so **we could be healed**.*
Isaiah 53:4-5

Jesus took on our weaknesses, our sorrows, our rebellion and our sin in exchange for His wholeness and healing. The prophet Isaiah called the coming Messiah the Prince of Peace. It is God's desire to give us peace but he won't force it on us. It's our choice. However, saying yes means facing the truth of all we've avoided, denied and minimized. Shame and secrecy have kept these things hidden. Now we intentionally choose to lay both aside in order to find healing and freedom. Remember, "The heart is deceitful above all things and beyond cure. Who can understand it?" (Jeremiah 17:9) We can never trust our own ability to honestly view our past, not now and not even after we've completed this journey. We will fall back into self-deception unless we learn to continually seek God's viewpoint while rejecting our own!

A Truthful Inventory of My Life

We can't find healing until we get honest. We get honest by doing an intentional, detailed inventory of our lives. To do this, we pause and ask God to help us see ourselves from His point of view. This can be scary. After all, some of us have spent the majority of our lives trying to avoid facing the truth.

Give Me Some Good Reasons I Should Do This

Let's review the principle:

I find healing when I face the truth of my life, inviting God's Spirit to reveal what I'm unable to see on my own.

The question is why? Why is the unexamined life not worth living?

> "Nothing paralyzes our souls more than working at hiding. We only allow others to come into the living room of our lives and no further. We keep the doors of the other rooms locked, sealing them off to prevent others from getting to know who we really are. We think by keeping them out that we're protecting ourselves, but in fact we are keeping ourselves locked in. We have built a prison for our souls."
> —Dr. Yolanda Lopez, Leadership & Development Pastor,
> CityChurch, San Antonio

This principle will help you sort through the confusion and contradiction of your life so that you can find out who you really are. You'll never be truly free until you rid yourself of the things that have controlled you. Then you can live the rich and satisfying life that Jesus promised all of us (John 10:10). Nothing you're about to face will surprise God. He knew every detail of your life when He chose to accept and love you.

> *O Lord, you have examined my heart and know everything about me. You know when I set down or stand up. You know my thoughts even when I'm far away. You see me when I travel and when I rest at home. You know everything I do. You know what I am going to say even before I say it, Lord. You go before me and follow me.*
> Psalm 139:1-5

The Need for an Accountability Partner/Mentor

At this point, we choose to quit lying to ourselves and others. We do this best when we have an accountability partner or mentor. This role is filled by a trusted friend who will listen to and encourage us as we work through the process. What is the difference between an accountability partner and a mentor? An accountability partner is someone (maybe someone in your group) who is also going through this healing process. A mentor is one who has completed the process. Either one can serve in this position.

Begin now to think through people you might select to serve as your accountability partner or mentor. It is best to choose a non-relative and someone of the same gender. Write down three possible names now. Pray that God will show you who to ask. (It is your responsibility to seek out and ask someone to fill this role.)

How Do I Complete a Truth Inventory?

Before beginning your inventory, review the first three principles then ask for God's help and guidance. You may want to use King David's prayer:

> *Search me, O God, and know my heart; test me and know my anxious thoughts. Point out anything in me that offends you, and lead me along the path of everlasting life.*

We do the truth search by examining all of our relationships, both past and current, targeting those that have been a source of resentment or fear and then those in which we have caused pain or harmed others. We will complete two lists: a resentment list and a harms list. (Several copies of both these lists are found in the Appendix section of this workbook. Feel free to make more copies as needed.)

Resentments List

WHO List people or groups that you resent or fear	WHAT Briefly state what they did that harmed you	HOW How did this affect you?	MY PART Where were you at fault in your words, thoughts or actions?	ACTION NEEDED Forgive/ Make Amends/ Set Boundaries
My father	He abandoned me and rejected me	I've always lowered my standards to keep a man in my life	Resentment and self-pity (I used this my entire life as an excuse to drink and drug)	Forgive him

1. In Column 1 of your Inventory Sheet (see sample above), write the names of people, groups, or institutions towards whom you have had feelings of fear or resentment. A short description will serve if you don't remember the name of the person or group involved. (For example: my mom or dad, my 3rd grade teacher, Elm Street neighbor, my ex-spouse or significant other, a coach, my boss at Tech World, men who used me.)

   Don't hurry. Give yourself time to think back over your life; then ask God to reveal any fears or resentments you have forgotten. Make this list as complete as you can, thinking through each decade for anyone (living or dead) towards whom you have felt resentment or fear. You will probably use several of these sheets.

   Important note: Include those you believe you've already forgiven if there's a possibility that you have minimized the effect their actions had on you.

2. In Column 2, write a short phrase describing what happened to make you angry or fearful. Think of this as a fact-finding mission—one word or a short phrase is sufficient. (Some examples: She humiliated me, he abandoned me, she didn't give me love or attention, he abused or molested me, she lied about me, or he stole from me.)

   It is best (and less stressful) to work through all of columns 1 & 2 to the best of your ability before going on to column 3.

3. Briefly explain how this action affected you. Did it affect your security needs, social needs, or sexuality? You'll find a list of Basic Needs in Appendix B to help you identify these.

4. In Column 4, we get honest about our responses to what happened. Ask yourself: "How was I at fault in my words, thoughts or actions?" Review the My Part list in Appendix C to help prompt accurate thoughts. Have I been judgmental, bitter, unforgiving, selfish, dishonest, or immoral? (Please note that the appropriate response to some harms done to us, especially those done to us as small children, may be to write the word "NONE" in this space.)

5. In Column 5, we make an action list. Do you need to forgive the person who hurt you? Do you need to make amends for your part in the conflict? Or do you simply need better boundaries between you and someone who has not respected you? If you're unsure, leave this column blank for now. We will complete this list a little further in our process.

*It's important to note that the goal of this inventory is the information in Columns 4 and 5. You will be using this information as you continue the process.

Harms List

WHO	WHAT	MY PART	MY BASIC NEEDS	ACTION NEEDED
List people or groups you've harmed physically, emotionally, verbally, financially, or sexually	Briefly state what you did or failed to do that caused harm	(Anger, broken promises, controlling, lying, lust, pride, etc.)	Which basic need drove this action?	Forgive/Make Amends/Set Boundaries
My kids	I was too depressed to meet their needs	Selfish, depressed, withholding love	Codependency, fear, selfishness	Make amends

1. When you've worked through the Resentments List, go to the Harms List (see sample above). In Column 1, list those you have harmed physically, emotionally, verbally, financially, or sexually. (Some examples: my ex, my kids, my parents, my employer, women I used/slept with, a business associate, myself, or God.)

2. In Column 2, briefly state what you did (or failed to do) that harmed them. (Examples: I was too selfish to meet their needs, I lied to them, I stole from them, I took advantage of them, or I broke my promises to them.)

3. In Column 3 list your part in what happened. What was the specific character flaw(s) that harmed the other person? (Use the Character Flaws list in Appendix D to help you think through possibilities.)

4. In Column 4, list the area of need that you believe was driving your behavior at the time. (Look over Appendix B for a list of possibilities).

5. Use Column 5 to make an action list for each person or group you harmed. Do you need to apologize? Make financial amends? Give time or money to someone with a similar need? (We will cover your choices more thoroughly in the chapter ahead on Amends.)

Important note! Over the next seven weeks, please continue to work on these two inventory lists outside of group. Group time will be reserved to explore the CORE ISSUES we all face under our struggles. (It is especially helpful to invite your mentor or accountability partner to check with you weekly to see how your inventories are progressing and to discuss any roadblocks you are facing.)

DISCUSSION QUESTIONS:

1. Do you feel you have thoroughly worked through the first three principles? Briefly describe them here:

2. Do you have an accountability partner or mentor? If not, have you asked God to provide someone? Have you approached that person with your request?

3. What kinds of feelings are you having as you work on this principle?

4. Are you facing any resistance to writing out your inventory? If so, what tools could you use to overcome this reluctance?

5. What is your attitude towards yourself as you work this principle? Are you able to be compassionate with yourself?

6. Can you see any humor in your past behaviors?

7. What are you like when you feel the best about yourself? (Be specific.)

8. Who has been a primary source of negative emotions in your life? (Consider feelings of resentment, anger, hurt, fear, grief, betrayal, rejection, jealousy, hatred, etc.) List names or identifying information here and transfer to Column 1 of your resentments list.

9. What did they do? (Be brief and specific.)

10. How did their actions affect you?

11. What area of your life was affected? (Consider your need for affection, security, approval, encouragement, respect, affirmation, and comfort.)

12. Did you make any negative choices that contributed to the situation?

4.1 Anger

Unresolved anger can sabotage any relationship. It did with Tom and Julie. Tom looked like he'd just been struck by lightning as he sat in front of me, tearfully telling his story. After 20 years, Julie had just told him she was filing for divorce. Tom didn't have a clue that things were that bad until he got home the day before and found the locks changed and his belongings in the garage. As Tom continued to talk, it became clear that he had grown up with a hypercritical, abusive mother and a distant father. He had never really felt loved or supported in anything he did. After four years in the Navy, he met and married Julie. Julie had been abandoned by her own mother and physically, emotionally and sexually abused by her new stepmother. When she met Tom she thought he was the answer to her prayers and that she'd finally be happy.

Although Tom was never physically abusive, his anger was expressed in one way or another almost every day. He was controlling, dominating, and critical. Julie had developed such low self-esteem from her childhood that she thought she deserved Tom's anger. When I spoke with Julie a few days later, she told me that she knew that God hated divorce and that it was a sin, but that she would simply die if she stayed with Tom any longer.

On the surface, Tom's anger appeared to be the problem, but actually *both* Tom and Julie had unresolved anger that ate away at their once happy marriage. Tom expressed his anger *outwardly* while Julie expressed hers *inwardly*. Julie's stuffing of her anger had kept Tom in the dark about how bad things were until her heart was so totally closed down that she could not or would not allow him another chance.

What about you? How has the anger of others affected your life? Have you adopted any un-healthy anger patterns yourself? Maybe, like Tom, you tend to blow up. Or maybe you're more like Julie and would never have thought of yourself as an angry person. If so, you may suffer from depression or physical symptoms. And what do you believe about anger? Is it a sin to be angry?

Over the next seven weeks (while you are continuing to work on your life inventory), we will begin to explore the *roots* of our junk—the layers that hide under our surface problems and strug-gles. Because it's so common, we'll begin with a deeper understanding of anger and then we'll examine some important core issues (unhealed wounds, unmet needs, pride, fear, and a distorted view of God).

Every day the evening news details the devastation of out-of-control anger—murder, violence, domestic disputes, child abuse—these and more come from angry hearts. Over the years, I've heard hundreds of stories of relational pain. Although anger is probably the factor that causes more of these problems than any other, most of us have little awareness of the role it plays.

Let's start with the basics. What can we know about anger in general? Is all anger sinful? If not, what makes the difference? We've already acknowledged that we live in a fallen world—a world that's been scarred by the effects of our own and others' sin. When things go wrong, we get angry!

Anger is as human as hunger and as unavoidable as pain. But it's important to understand that anger can either be a *sinful response* or a *response to sin*.

Anger can either be a *sinful response* or a *response to sin*

"Don't sin by letting anger control you." Don't let the sun go down
while you are still angry, for anger gives a foothold to the devil.
Ephesians 4:26-28

Anger as a Response to Sin

1. Anger is an *appropriate* response to evil. Jesus responded to evil with anger and at least once with actual violence:

> *In the Temple area he saw merchants selling cattle, sheep, and doves for sacrifices; he also saw dealers at tables exchanging foreign money. Jesus made a whip from some ropes and chased them all out of the Temple. He drove out the sheep and cattle, scattered the money changers' coins over the floor, and turned over their tables. Then, going over to the people who sold doves, he told them, "Get these things out of here. Stop turning my Father's house into a marketplace!"*
> John 2:14-16

2. Anger can be a healthy protest when we are threatened physically or emotionally by the sinful choices of others. It can be a warning signal for the soul in much the same way that pain is for the body.

Anger as a Sinful Response

1. Old, stored anger is always toxic. If you put a clean trash bag in a new trash can then added a box of crispy fried chicken, could you safely eat it? Sure. But walk away and leave that chicken for a week and there's no way. Now it's rotted and full of maggots. The only factor that changed was time. Even righteous anger will turn into toxic anger if left unresolved:

> *You must all be quick to listen, slow to speak, and slow to get angry. Human anger does not produce the righteousness God desires.*
> James 1:19-20

2. Toxic anger is the number one destroyer of in-love feelings:

> *A fool gives full vent to his anger, but a wise man keeps himself under control.*
> Proverbs 29:11

3. Anger will control us until we stop blaming others for our angry feelings and admit that it is a choice for which we alone are responsible. God warned Cain about this before he killed his brother:

> *"You will be accepted if you do what is right. But if you refuse to do what is right, then watch out! Sin is crouching at the door, eager to control you. But you must subdue it and be its master."*
> Genesis 4:7

A Definition of Anger

In *The Anger Workbook,* Les Carter & Frank Minirth define anger as "the emotion we experience when three things are threatened: our *personal worth,* our *essential needs,* or our *basic convictions.*"

I like to think of anger as a protest against an unwanted event. It can be either healthy or unhealthy. Let's start by looking at the three unhealthy expressions of anger: aggressive, suppressed, and passive-aggressive.

Three Unhealthy Expressions of Anger

1. **Aggressive Anger**
   Those of us who express our anger aggressively are prone to blow up without regard to the feelings of others. We *know* we're angry, but are likely to blame the way we feel on the behavior of those around us. We may express our frustration through any of the following: yelling, criticizing, throwing things, blaming, intimidating, hitting or controlling. We have a lot of stored anger and all it takes is a small trigger to set it off. Like Tom, the family of someone with aggressive anger learns to tiptoe around him/her, doing their best to prevent another blow-up.

2. **Suppressed Anger**
   Those of us who suppress our anger can seem calm enough on the outside. Instead of letting our anger out, we push it down deep inside us. We are uncomfortable with any outward expression of anger and often suffer from emotional symptoms like depression or anxiety and physical symptoms like headaches, insomnia, or digestive problems. As children, we may have been intimidated by the anger of someone close to us. Or we may have been punished when we tried to express an opinion. Like Julie, those who suppress are often unaware that they even *have* an anger problem.

   It's not unusual for the anger of a suppressor to be expressed in obsessive-compulsive behavior and perfectionism. Lots of people tell me that they never get angry. When I hear that phrase, I almost always find that I'm facing a Suppressor. When anger is unresolved, it is buried alive and grows inside us like cancer. It creates more and more darkness inside our hearts. This darkness creates distance between us and both God and others. It can cause migraines, ulcers, high blood pressure, and insomnia. You are six times more likely to have a heart attack when you have stored anger.

3. **Passive Aggressive Anger**
   Those of us who express our anger through passive aggression direct our anger outward but instead of blowing up, we resort to more subtle punishing tactics like sulking, sarcasm, procrastination, eye-rolling, stubbornness, and the silent treatment. We know we're angry, but aren't willing to take the risk of confronting. Our goal is to make the person we're angry with feel sorry for how he or she treated us without owning our own actions.

Three Healthy Expressions of Anger

If *how* we handle our anger is the key, what are some healthy ways it can be expressed? The Bible gives us three strategies for resolving every form of our anger: confronting our offenders, forgiving our offenders, and overlooking the offense.

1. **Confronting Our Offenders**

   When we confront our offenders, we use assertive anger to confront them with a desire to restore the relationship and resolve the issue without harming the other person. The Bible calls this "speaking the truth in love." Jesus said:

   > *"If another believer sins against you, go privately and point out*
   > *the offense. If the other person listens and confesses it, you have*
   > *won that person back. But if you are unsuccessful, take one or two*
   > *others with you and go back again, so that everything you say may*
   > *be confirmed by two or three witnesses. If the person still refuses to*
   > *listen, take your case to the church. Then if he or she won't*
   > *accept the church's decision, treat that person as a pagan*
   > *or a corrupt tax collector."*
   > Matthew 18:15-17

   Use confrontation when the other person is a someone who respects the opinions and rights of others and when harm will result if no change is made.

2. **Forgiving Our Offenders**

   Forgiveness is the remedy for anger caused by most serious offenses. Whether or not we confront, we need to give up our right to hold the offense against the other person. Forgiving does not mean what happened was okay. It does not let the other person off the hook. It just transfers the right to judge them to God who can handle it in a much better manner than we can.

   > *Make allowance for each other's faults, and forgive anyone*
   > *who offends you. Remember, the Lord forgave you,*
   > *so you must forgive others.*
   > Colossians 3:13

   Forgiveness is actually a gift to ourselves! It releases us from the prison of our anger. (A little later in the process, we will take an entire chapter to examine the importance of forgiving others.)

3. **Overlooking the Offense**

   Realizing we have a list of our own imperfections allows us to overlook many offenses in others. A good rule of thumb in intimate relationships is to confront about 10% of the things that bug us and to overlook about 90%. (Some of us overlook almost everything. We are unwilling to confront no matter how important the issue. We need to learn to speak up about important issues. Others of us nit-pick almost everything. We love to correct others. We need to learn the skill of over-looking common irritations.)

   > *A person's wisdom yields patience;*
   > *it is to one's glory to overlook an offense.*
   > Proverbs 19:11

Core Issues

The following chart helps us understand how anger and the other issues in the outer circle are actually SYMPTOMS that are fed by one or more of four core issues. The core issues we all need to examine are: pride, fear, unmet needs, and unhealed wounds. Under those is the even deeper core issue of a distorted view of God.

CORE ISSUES

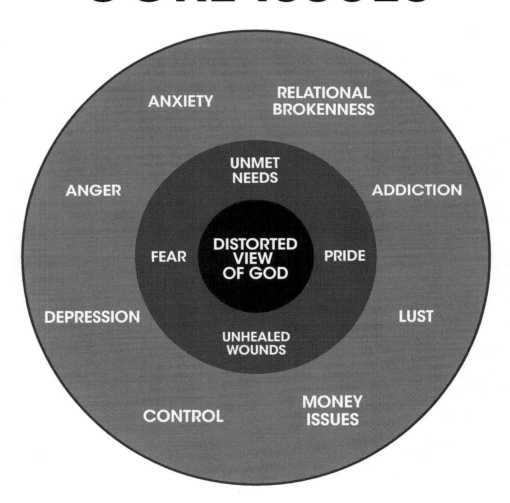

*The Core Issues Chart was developed by Pastors David Saathoff, Brent Saathoff, and Miriam Callahan.

DISCUSSION QUESTIONS:

1. How does your anger most often express itself? Are you more likely to express it aggressively, suppress it, or let it out passive-aggressively?

2. How have you been affected by the anger of others, especially those closest to you?

3. How has unresolved anger worked against you and those closest to you? Give specific examples:

4. Which of the Core Issues do you see evidence of in your life?

4.2 Pride

"If anyone would like to acquire humility, I can, I think, tell him the first step. The first step is to realize that one is proud."
— C.S. Lewis

When we get honest about our junk, we begin to admit that we are far from perfect. We struggle with issues like anger, depression, jealousy, gossip, addiction, anxiety, OCD, lying, judging others, lust—even hatred and violence. This is a BIG step in the right direction. These things can easily appear to be our main problem. They hurt us and they hurt others. But we have found they are merely *symptoms* of deeper issues. If we are ever to get truly free, we'll need to examine the CORE ISSUES that feed our surface issues.

**The layer under our junk is made up of four CORE issues:
pride, fear, unmet needs, and unhealed wounds as well as the deeper
HARD CORE issue of a distorted view of God.**

The first CORE issue we'll examine is PRIDE.

One of the most powerful examples of the danger of living in pride comes from the Old Testament book of Daniel. King Nebuchadnezzar ruled in Babylon during the time of Israel's exile. His kingdom and his fame were great. While our hero Daniel was serving as royal counselor, King Nebuchadnezzar had a disturbing dream—one that foretold God's judgment on his prideful heart. Daniel warned Nebuchadnezzar that he would "be driven from human society, and you will live in the fields with the wild animals. You will eat grass like a cow, and you will be drenched with the dew of heaven."

Just twelve months later, King Nebuchadnezzar was admiring all he'd accomplished and said, "Look at this great city of Babylon! By my own mighty power, I have built this beautiful city as my real residence to display my majestic splendor." No sooner had these words left his lips than the judgment was fulfilled and Nebuchadnezzar was driven from human society. He actually did eat grass like a cow and was drenched with the dew of heaven for seven long years. After this painful lesson, Nebuchadnezzar lifted his eyes toward heaven and his sanity was restored. His change of heart became evident as he praised the God of Daniel with these words:

*"Now I, Nebuchadnezzar, praise and glorify and honor
the King of heaven. All His acts are just and true, and
He is able to humble the proud."*
Daniel 4:37

Nebuchadnezzar's pride had caused him to take all the credit for his success. Pride is listed as the root sin that caused Lucifer's fall from the presence of God:

*"I ordained and anointed you as the mighty angelic guardian. You had
access to the holy mountain of God and walked among the stones of
fire. Your heart was filled with pride because of all your beauty. Your
wisdom was corrupted by your love of splendor. So I threw you to the
ground and exposed you to the curious gaze of kings."*
Ezekiel 28:14, 17

And the Bible puts pride at the top of God's hate list:

> *"I hate pride and arrogance,*
> *corruption and perverse speech."*
> Proverbs 8:13

In God's view, pride seems to be at *epidemic* proportions in the human race.

Pride is More Than Arrogance

For years I struggled with what I saw as a conflict between my observation of people and the Bible's emphasis on pride. What I observed was an epidemic of *low self-esteem*, not high. Yet I couldn't discount the many biblical warnings I saw against the sin of pride. That's when it dawned on me—at its core, pride is really an unhealthy focus on SELF.

Yes, it can look like arrogance, but it can also look like self-reliance, self-pity and even self-condemnation. Classic Christian author Oswald Chambers called pride "the deification of self." Pride is a hidden root that puts self on the throne of our lives and creates a wall between us and the healing, love and blessing of God.

> **Pride is an unhealthy focus on SELF**

When pride is working in my life, I am unable to see myself realistically. I may see myself as better than others or I may believe I'm the only one I can rely on. I may even see myself as worthless and inferior. In any case, this self-distortion is greatly damaging my life and my relationships and preventing me from living the abundant life Jesus promised. Thinking of it in this way, it is apparent that pride is a *universal* human pitfall.

Let's look at all three faces of pride.

The Three Faces of Pride

1. **Self-absorption**
   This is the "me first" face of pride. Self-absorption says, "If I don't look out for me, no one will." It means taking what you think you need without regard to the needs or feelings of others. Self-absorption was lurking each time we manipulated others to get what we wanted. How often have you demanded your own way—from how things are done around your house, to where you'll go to eat, to how you'll spend (or not spend) money? Look under self-absorption and you'll often find this fear: "my needs won't be met if I don't stay in control and MAKE you do the right thing." Self-absorption uses guilt or anger to manipulate others to get its way. It disregards one of the most important gifts God gave us—the free will of others. Toddlers and teens are notorious for being self-absorbed. But self-absorption can become a character flaw that leaks over into adult life.

   Those who struggle with this distortion can see themselves as more important or better than others. Arrogance leaks out in both their attitude and comments towards others they regard as below them. Do you ever make yourself feel more important by putting others down?

2. **Self-reliance**
   Self-reliance says, "I don't need anyone, I'm fine." This more subtle form of pride refuses to depend on others. It attempts to motivate us with unrealistically high expectations. "You

should"and "you ought" are its mottos. God was deliberate in warning His people of the danger of falling into self-reliant pride:

> *For when you have become full and prosperous and have built fine homes to live in, and when your flocks and herds have become very large and your silver and gold have multiplied along with everything else, be careful! Do not become proud at the time and forget the Lord your God, who rescued you from slavery in the land of Egypt...* *He did all this* [miraculously provided] *so you would never say to yourself, 'I have achieved this wealth with my own strength and energy.'*
> Deuteronomy 8:12-14, 17

3. **Self-condemnation**

Self-condemnation is the third face of pride. Self-condemnation says, "I'm no good, not even God could love me!" Self still demands attention even though it's *negative* attention. Under self-condemnation lie shame, self-rejection and self-bitterness. It repels God's love and the love of others with feelings of unworthiness. In self-condemnation, we stubbornly refuse to forgive ourselves and are willing to tolerate evil behavior on the part of those around us due to our fear of rejection. Listen to Mary's story:

> I spent almost thirty years being deceived about who I was at the core. I was brought up believing that I was completely worthless. Every day I heard statements like: "You will never amount to anything," "you are retarded," "you had a talent and threw it away, now God will never give you another one," and even "you are the devil's child"! My parents' statements became my self-image. Self-condemnation shaped everything about my life, from the places I went to the choices I made. After months of healing, God has changed those deceptive thoughts. Now I understand that God sees me as His child, completely forgiven. I don't have to prove my worth to anyone. God says I am His child and that makes me special and worth it!

What are the symptoms of self-condemnation?

- Comparison
- Excessive competition
- Self-abuse (overeating, anorexia, cutting, harmful habits)
- Self-accusation (perfectionism, performance-based acceptance, people-pleasing)
- Self-pity
- Self-sabotage
- Codependency
- Rejecting others and being rejected

To what degree is pride affecting your life? Take the following test to find out:

The Pride Test

___I get angry when things don't go my way.

___I can't trust anyone but myself to get things done right.

___I often have negative thoughts about myself.

___I frequently focus on the failings of others.

___Sometimes I fantasize what life would be like if I could have ideal circumstances.

___Most people would say I have a strong personality.

___I am not known for saying "I was wrong."

___I rarely let others see my true self.

___I am offended by honest criticism.

___I demand that my rights be respected.

___I often blame others for my problems.

___I will do whatever it takes to avoid being seen as weak.

___I honestly believe I am better than certain other groups of people.

___I have been known to sulk when things did not go my way.

___I demand that others meet my needs.

___I rarely notice when others are having a bad day.

___I'm not good at affirming or encouraging others.

___I have difficulty accepting others faults.

___It's hard for me to admit my weaknesses and limitations.

___It's hard for me to listen for any length of time when others speak about subjects I care nothing about.

___It's important to follow the rules even if someone gets hurt.

___I find myself telling 'white lies' to avoid trouble.

___Winning is very important to me.

___My hobbies take up more of my time than my loved ones would like.

___I'm good at persuading others to see things my way.

___When dining out with relatives, friends or co-workers, I tend to choose where we'll eat.

___I feel unworthy.

___When I give to others, I expect something in return.

___**Total**

If you checked ten or more items, you may struggle with pride. If you checked fifteen or more, pride is likely a core issue for you. (A person who struggles with pride is by nature blind to his own pride. To get the best insight into your pride level, have your spouse or close friend or family member complete this test for you.)

*The Pride Test was created by Miriam Callahan and Dr. Brent Saathoff.

Humility: The Antidote for Pride

Humility is God's potent antidote for every form of pride. Since it's the polar opposite of pride, we can think of humility as a *healthy* view of self. When we live in true humility, we will neither *overinflate* nor *underinflate* our view of ourselves. We can see ourselves as the most valuable of all God's creations, but also know that we aren't capable of existing outside of dependence on God.

Humility invites God's blessing and help in all we do:

> *And all of you, serve each other in humility, for*
> *"God opposes the proud but favors the humble."*
> 1 Peter 5:5

How can we move from pride to humility? There are four intentional paths that will decrease pride and increase humility in your life.

Four Intentional Paths to Decrease Pride and Increase Humility

Path 1: Humbling Yourself

God has given us the ability to choose to humble ourselves. And Jesus gave us an example to follow:

> *Don't be selfish; don't try to impress others. Be humble, thinking*
> *of others as better than yourselves. Don't look out only for your*
> *own interests, but take an interest in others, too. You must have the*
> *same attitude that Christ Jesus had. Though He was God, He did*
> *not think of equality with God as something to cling to. Instead,*
> *He gave up His divine privileges; He took the humble position of a*
> *slave and was born as a human being.*
> *When He appeared in human form, He humbled Himself in*
> *obedience to God and died a criminal's death on a cross.*
> *Therefore, God elevated Him to the place of highest honor and gave*
> *Him the name above all other names.*
> Philippians 2:3-9

Humbling yourself begins with admitting to both God and to others that you've been wrong.

> *So admit to one another that you have sinned.*
> *Pray for one another so that you might be healed.*
> James 5:16 (NIRV)

Path 2: Brokenness

The second path is often the most painful. It can come upon us suddenly through major life losses such as loss of career, status, or marriage. But we can also choose the path of brokenness. We can choose to invite God to show us every shred of impurity or bitterness that's been stored in our hearts. Those who experience this path have learned the secret of increased intimacy with God:

The LORD is close to the brokenhearted;
He rescues those whose spirits are crushed.
Psalm 34:18

Path 3: Requesting Feedback

We can look for a trusted friend and then invite that person to be honest with us about our strengths as well as our weaknesses. While we are actively working through this transformation process, we have asked an accountability partner to serve in that role. That's good. But it's wise to continue to invite that kind of honesty throughout our lives.

Wounds from a sincere friend are better than
many kisses from an enemy.
Proverbs 27:6

Path 4: Serving Others

Jesus reversed the pecking order that we so often see in society. He called us to reject that kind of thinking by choosing to serve rather than be served:

… Jesus called them together and said, "You know that the rulers
in this world lord it over their people, and officials flaunt their
authority over those under them. But among you it
will be different. Whoever wants to be a leader among you
must be your servant, and whoever wants to be first among you
must be the slave to everyone else. For even the Son of Man
came not to be served but to serve others and to give His
life as a ransom for many."
Mark 10:42-45

A Prayer to Release Self-absorption and Self-reliance

Dear Heavenly Father, I see now that I've been guilty of sins of selfishness and self-reliance. I have allowed myself to take your place on the throne of my heart. In the name of Jesus, and as an act of my free will, I confess and renounce these areas of pride that I've tolerated in my heart. Please forgive me.

I cancel Satan's authority over me because I have also chosen to forgive myself.
In the powerful name of Jesus, I command every spirit of pride to leave me now. Holy Spirit, I invite you to come into my heart to heal me of the effects of pride.
Give me more and more humility as I continue through life.
In Jesus' name, Amen.

A Prayer to Renounce a Negative Self-image

Father, I choose to believe the truth that I am chosen and loved by you. I choose to believe that I am no longer under the curse of the law because Christ became a curse for me. I renounce the lie that _____ (specific negative words). I announce the truth that my identity and sense of worth is found in who I am as your child. I renounce seeking the approval and acceptance of other people and I choose to believe that I have been saved, not by what I have done, but by your mercy and grace. By your grace, Heavenly Father, I choose from this day forward to walk by faith in the power of your Holy Spirit according to what *you* have said is true.
In Jesus' name, Amen.

A Prayer to Release Self-condemnation

Dear Heavenly Father, in the name of Jesus, and as an act of my free will, I confess and renounce the areas of self-condemnation that I've tolerated in my heart. In the name of Jesus and by the power of His blood, I forgive myself for every way I've ever failed God. I release myself from any guilt and shame attached. I cancel Satan's authority over me because I have now chosen to forgive myself. In the powerful name of Jesus, I command the spirit of self-condemnation to leave me now. Holy Spirit, I invite you to come into my heart to heal me of the effects of self-condemnation. Give me more and more humility as I continue through life.
In Jesus' name, Amen.

DISCUSSION QUESTIONS:

1. At what times in your life have you been stubborn, selfish or looked down on others to make yourself feel better? Have you thought of this as pride?

2. How and when have you been guilty of relying on yourself instead of on God?

3. What are your thoughts as you gaze into a mirror?

4. What signs of self-condemnation do you see in your life?

5. What are some of the negative messages you heard growing up?

6. For what things do you find it most difficult to forgive yourself?

7. Humility is the antidote for pride. Have you chosen any of the four paths to greater humility (brokenness, humbling yourself, requesting feedback, serving others)? Describe them:

4.3 Fear

Fear is a powerful negative motivator. Billionaire Warren Buffett and Pastor Joel Osteen each had a terrifying fear of public speaking. So did I. I avoided taking my college's freshman speech class three years in a row. As a senior I had no choice but to suffer through the class if I wanted to graduate, so I finally did. My fear of public speaking continued to limit my choices until 2005. That's when I came to see this fear as a failure to trust God and a refusal to use the authority he had given me to reject and evict my fears. I had believed and had taught others that fear is an emotion—that we could control only our thoughts and behaviors, not our emotions. But as I read a small book called *Recognizing Your Spiritual Authority* by John Bevere, I realized that fear can be more than just an emotion, it can also be a *spirit*. I learned that we have been given the right to choose to trust God as well as the right to reject and evict the spirit of fear from our hearts. That day I asked God to forgive me for not trusting him and I rejected every spirit of fear, using Jesus' name. Fear left me that very day. I've been free to speak (and to pray for others before I speak) ever since!

As we search for the roots that feed our surface issues we will often find that fear has been residing inside us, influencing our thoughts, emotions, and choices. Look for fear under surface issues of control, perfectionism, excessive talking, worry, insecurity, anxiety, and anger. For many of us, fear in one form or another has become a way of life. We may medicate ourselves in order to be able to function, but fear remains. If we are to be truly free, we must take the time to expose and examine our fears.

How has fear limited or affected your life?

Let's look at three kinds of fears and how they may be adversely affecting us.

Three Kinds of Harmful Fear

1. **A Lifestyle of Stress and Anxiety**
    Although God gave us the fight-or-flight response to deal with temporary emergencies, he designed our bodies and souls to live in a state of peace called homeostasis. The problem comes when we begin to *exist* in an elevated state of stress or anxiety. We never quite settle down into homeostasis or peace. My friend Ish Payne calls this "Living in the Red Zone." Ish created the Red Zone Chart to help us grasp our dilemma:

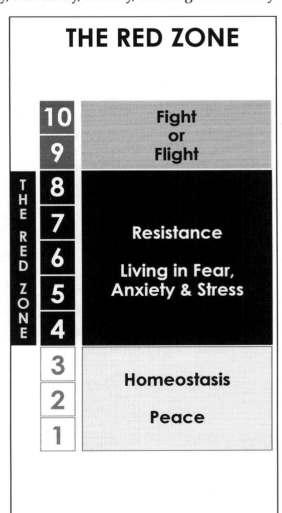

*Taken with permission from *Life in the Red Zone,* Restoring Hearts Ministries, 2006.

When we go into the Fight or Flight response, massive amounts of adrenaline and cortisol are triggered, accounting for the extra strength necessary to fight for our lives or to rescue a loved one. As the crisis ends, we go through a stage called "resistance." During this 20 to 60 minute period, the body gradually returns to its pre-arousal levels. If all is well, we return to our original state of homeostasis or peace. This is a God-given response, occurring across cultural, gender, and racial lines.

Our problem begins when we *exist* in a state of chronic stress or anxiety. What can move you into this zone? Worry, guilt, strife, bitterness, and fears of all kinds—just to name a few. Red Zone living not only affects the emotions and thoughts—it takes a heavy toll on the body. The constant production of adrenaline and cortisol which *helped* us in the flight-or-flight mode now begin to harm our body's systems. Jesus wanted His followers to avoid this trap. He talked about the temptation to live in a state of worry.

> *"I tell you, do not worry...can you add even one hour to your life*
> *by worrying? And why do you worry about clothes? Your faith is*
> *so small! So don't worry...put God's kingdom first. Do what He*
> *wants you to do. Then all of those things will also be given to you.*
> *So don't worry about tomorrow. Tomorrow will worry about itself.*
> *Each day has enough trouble of its own."*
> Matthew 6:25-34

Living without Margin

When we live on the edge of our financial, emotional, physical, and mental resources, we are setting ourselves up for Red Zone living. This happens when the fear of failure drives us to perform at an unhealthy level. Nothing is ever quite enough. We may hear praise for our time and energy investments, but they never satisfy the expectation we carry for ourselves. Soon after Israel's miraculous exodus from Egypt, Moses fell into this trap. Day after day, Moses alone listened to the problems of every single Hebrew citizen.

> *"This is not good!" Moses' father-in-law exclaimed. "You're going*
> *to wear yourself out—and the people, too. This job is too heavy a*
> *burden for you to handle all by yourself."*
> Exodus 18:17-18

2. The Fear of Man

The Bible describes a problem of over-concern with what others think, calling it the "fear of man." Fear of man causes us to value the opinions of others over God's opinion:

> *Fear of man will prove to be a snare,*
> *but whoever trusts in the LORD is kept safe.*
> Proverbs 29:25

Some of us have sacrificed our morals and even the health of our own souls due to fear of losing someone we love. In modern terms, fear of man is called people-pleasing. Why would anyone lower their standards and tolerate the intolerable in those close to them? Fear of rejection is the fuel for this behavior.

And people-pleasing is no small matter in God's eyes. God removed Saul (the first king of Israel) from the throne because he chose to please others over obeying God. Listen as the prophet Samuel confronts Saul:

> *"Why did you not obey the LORD? Why did you pounce on the*
> *plunder and do evil in the eyes of the LORD?" Then Saul said to*
> *Samuel, "I have sinned. I violated the LORD's command and your*
> *instructions. I was afraid of the people and so I gave in to them."*
> *But Samuel replied, "I will not go back with you! Since you have*
> *rejected the Lord's command, He has rejected you as king of Israel."*
> 1 Samuel 15:19, 24, 26

3. Specific Fears or Phobias

We live in a sin-filled world—a world that has been controlled since the Garden of Eden by the choices of the people who inhabit it. Abuse and misuse as well as exposure to traumatic life events can create a fear response in the human heart. It's not too much to say that fear of one type or another is normal for those living outside the healing of God and intentional dependency on him.

Does Good Fear Exist?

God is constantly reassuring his fearful children with the words: "Do not fear." It's a constant refrain in both Old and New Testaments.

> *"I am the God of your father Abraham.*
> *Do not be afraid, for I am with you…"*
> Genesis 26:24

> *"So do not fear, for I am with you;*
> *do not be dismayed, for I am your God."*
> Isaiah 41:10

It seems that fear is a *bad* thing. So is there such a thing as a *good* fear? God invites us to live with only *one* fear. He says it's the only fear that will bring blessing and good into our lives. In the Bible, this fear is called the 'fear of the Lord.' King Solomon, the wisest man who ever lived, had these thoughts on the subject:

> *Now all has been heard; here is the conclusion of the matter:*
> *fear God and keep His commandments,*
> *for this is the whole duty of man.*
> Ecclesiastes 12:13

God gives us his promise that we *can* live in peace. It happens as we learn to trust and keep our eyes on him.

> *You will keep in perfect peace all who trust in you, all whose*
> *thoughts are fixed on you! Trust in the Lord always, for the Lord*
> *God is the eternal Rock.*
> Isaiah 26:3-4

We don't need to fear anything or anyone other than God because God's power is stronger than any power on earth.

A further look will reveal promises of God's love, righteousness, physical provision and wisdom awaiting those who live with the fear of God in the face of life's threats (See Psalm 103:17, Psalm 111:5, and Psalm 111:10).

Honesty requires a clear assessment of the levels of fear that reside in our hearts. Is your life full of unnecessary stress? Do you live in worry or anxiety? Have you experienced unhealed trauma or abuse resulting in phobias or fears? Do you drive yourself to perform, always setting the bar just a little too high to reach?

In this part of our journey, our part is to admit what we find. Admitting the truth is half the battle. We can't fix ourselves but we *can* be intentional about bringing what we've found to God for healing. Only God can remove fear and bring healing to the hidden places of our hearts.

A Prayer to Defeat Fear

Father, in your wisdom you have commanded me
to fear you and you alone.
I have allowed my heart to fear many things other than you.
In the name of Jesus Christ, I ask you to forgive me for failing to
trust you completely. I come to you with my fearful heart.
Please heal me and set me free from all remaining fear.
By an act of my will, I now choose to place all of my trust in you.
I desire to lean on you from this day forward. I know that you have
promised to give me your perfect peace as I do this.
In Jesus' name, Amen.

DISCUSSION QUESTIONS:

1. How have the three harmful fears (a lifestyle of stress and anxiety, fear of man, and specific or acute fears or phobias) affected you?

2. How much time do you spend living in the Red Zone? How?

3. In what ways do you practice the fear of the Lord?

4.4 Unmet Needs

Nearly every week I meet men and women who struggle with a wide variety of surface issues—issues like anger, fear of failure, or control. Although they often look great on the outside, below the surface lies a common root. All of them grew up in an emotionally cold environment. This is how Laura tells her story:

> My name is Laura and I am a wife, a daughter, a sister, a friend, and finally just a worship leader. I struggle with the need to be accepted by others and with building strong personal ties with my family and friends. I struggle with belonging and with showing and feeling love. Growing up, my family did not show or speak words of affection for one another. That was just how it was. Love was shown through provision, security and rules. My father is of Polish descent (Catholic background) and my mother is of Chinese descent (Buddhist background.) That information alone lets you know of the high standards that were prevalent in my family. One important rule was to respect everyone else, sometimes at the cost of yourself. School grades had to be very high. Career choices should be becoming a doctor, lawyer, or at least being financially successful. I don't think I ever saw my parents kiss or say that they loved one another. I don't remember any cuddling, tickling, or much laughing. I have two brothers that got into trouble left and right, so I learned fast what not to say or do and I quickly erected walls around my heart that were not easily penetrable. Please don't get me wrong, my family loves each other, but a basic need was neglected. The lack of love and belonging I experienced stunted me severely. God began the destruction of that wall on a plane ride back from a mission trip. We had just ministered to kids in an orphanage in the eastern European nation of Moldova. Little did I know that the God of the Universe had begun a work in my life that would reverse the lack of affection in our family.
>
> On the long flight back, Pastor Doug Robins asked me how the trip was going. I told him that I couldn't fathom a particular interaction with a young Moldovan girl that freely embraced me and said in broken English, "I love you." I struggled with her saying something so intimate to someone she hardly even knew. Pastor Doug was led by the Spirit of God to immediately pass me to Pastor Miriam for counsel. Pretty soon thereafter Miriam and I were embracing, right there in the middle of the aisle of the plane! We prayed and cried for an hour. Seriously, we embraced for an hour. That was so hard for me. I couldn't run or hide. There were people all around us probably thinking how crazy we were. But God demolished the wall I had built around my heart and swept me up into a Level 5, Hand of God Love Tornado, and I've been in it ever since!
>
> I still work not to build up that wall again. But my family, my marriage, and my friendships are WAY better than I could ever imagine. God still holds me in His arms and doesn't let go for anything. I am a little girl when I am in His arms. He is my Daddy. I can honestly say that was the beginning of allowing God to truly love me."

Emotionally cold families *look* perfectly normal—the parents may not have been particularly angry or abusive or addicted, but the children grew up without the warmth of their parent's approval, respect and even affection. Maybe that's you. You may not have thought of this as a CORE issue, but you know that growing up you received very little in the way of warmth and tenderness. Why is this so important? Because only a voluntary act of love can meet our needs.

Christian counselor David Ferguson tells the story of a mother who came to him in frustration. Her five-year-old daughter was so clingy that she refused to leave her mother's side, even to play with her toys. Dr. Ferguson suggested that the mom intentionally sit on the floor for 15 minutes every morning, giving the child her full attention. When she returned 7 days later, the mom had an amazing report. She said, "I don't know what happened but Lucy is like a different child! She no longer clings to me and has even started playing in her room alone!" Dr. Ferguson said, "that's because it's only when others *voluntarily* give to us that our needs can be met."

When we must work to get our needs met (by demanding attention or love or affection), it's as if there's a hole in our love bucket. The attention we force others to give us seems to just drain out.

> **When we must work to get our needs met, it's as if there's a hole in our love bucket**

Unmet needs are difficult for most of us to acknowledge because it's not about what *happened* to us—it's about what *didn't happen*! It's about not getting what we needed to thrive. We get honest when we evaluate the extent to which we had the following needs met in childhood:

Leftover Needs from Childhood

___ Love

___ Affection

___ Attention

___ Respect

___ Security

___ Belonging

___ Comfort

___ Encouragement

___ Discipline/Boundaries

___ To Be Known

___ To Know God

It's important to note that from birth to age two, our mother's role is to welcome us to life and to give us a sense of belonging. Our father's primary role (most vital from age two to six) is to give us a sense of identity and importance. Were your parents physically and emotionally present and equipped to invest in you at those ages?

We can survive but *we will not thrive* without having these needs met. Anger, depression, perfectionism, as well as sexual, food, and chemical addiction are common results of living for years with unmet needs.

Need Substitutes

What if we did not receive these basic needs in our childhood? How might we have tried to cope without them? Here are four primary substitutes people use to compensate for unmet needs:

- People (trying to find people that will finally accept and love us)
- Pleasure (food, sex, drugs, gambling)
- Performance (academic degrees, athletic success, or skills)
- Possessions

Substitutes can never truly meet the need of our hearts. Using these sets up a destructive cycle in our thoughts, feelings and behaviors. Here's how the cycle works:

The Destructive Cycle of Unmet Needs:

Needs Unmet ➤ Faulty Thinking ➤ Negative Feelings ➤
Unhealthy Behaviors ➤ Painful Outcomes

*Taken from *Relational First Aid* by Dr. David Ferguson.

When I expect to receive something from an unreliable source, I set myself up for constant disappointment. If this sounds like your life, is there anything you can do about it?

Four Steps for Healing Unmet Needs

1. **Admit the need exists and then ask God to forgive you for trying to meet your own needs.**

   "My people have done two things wrong. They have abandoned me,
   the fountain of life-giving water.
   They have also dug their own cisterns,
   broken cisterns that can't hold water."
   Jeremiah 2:13

2. **Grieve the reality that you may never receive the love you need from those who should have given it to you voluntarily.**

   Even if my father and mother abandon me,
   the Lord will hold me close.
   Psalm 27:10

3. **Stop going to an empty well for water.**

   Don't put your trust in mere humans. They are frail as breath.
   What good are they?
   Isaiah 2:22

4. Give God permission to heal your heart and fill you with His perfect love:

> *Not that I was ever in need, for I have learned how to be content*
> *with whatever I have. I know how to live on almost nothing*
> *or with everything. I have learned the secret of living in every*
> *situation, whether it is with a full stomach or empty,*
> *with plenty or little. For I can do everything through Christ,*
> *who gives me strength.*
> Philippians 4:6-7, 11-13

> *Each time He said, "My grace is all you need.*
> *My power works best in weakness."*
> *So now I am glad to boast about my weaknesses,*
> *so that the power of Christ can work through me.*
> 2 Corinthians 12:9

Are you willing to reject all the substitutes you have used? Only you can choose to position yourself as a child, looking to God as your only Source, your only Provider, and your only Comfort. If you are willing, here is a prayer to get you started.

A Prayer for Childlikeness

Father God, I choose now to come to you as a child.
I give up my attempts to meet my own needs and fix my eyes on
you alone as my Provider, my Source and my Comfort.
You are familiar with every empty place inside me.
Please come and fill me now with your love and healing.
In Jesus' name, Amen.

DISCUSSION QUESTIONS:

1. Look at the list of Leftover Needs from Childhood on page 57. Which of these needs were met in your childhood? Which were met only partially or not at all?

2. Which of the four primary patterns of focus or addiction (People, Pleasure, Performance or Possessions) did you use as substitutes for these needs? Give specific examples.

3. Have you ever set yourself up for disappointment by expecting to receive love, attention, or respect from an unreliable source? Describe.

4. What could you do differently now?

4.5 Unhealed Wounds

Unhealed wounds are a major source of our surface issues. That may sound obvious but sometimes it is completely blocked from our awareness. Let's begin by listening to Eva's story:

"My name is Eva and I was raised in a home where there was violence. Everything depended on whether Papa came home a happy drunk or an angry one. We had to be in bed every night at 8:30. Sometimes he was home by then, but many times he wasn't. My sister and I shared a bedroom right by the dining room and we knew it was going to be a bad night if Papa wasn't happy with the meal my mother had made and threw it across the room. Then the physical violence began. My mother and my brother got the worst of it. My father never touched us—he just scared us severely. If it got really bad, my mother would grab the three of us kids and walk about a mile to the fire station where she'd use the phone to call our grandfather. He would pick us up and we'd stay with him for a few days until Papa would come ask for forgiveness and beg my mother to come home. She went back every time even though we would cry and beg her not to go back. This happened many times until we got older and my brother could fight back.

During the H2O process, I found that all my anger was directed towards my mother. She was the one and only person who could have removed us from the situation but she always went back. Why? Why would she take the abuse and allow my brother to be abused? Why?

One day God brought back to my mind something I'd found out in my late teens. My mother had had a family before us that no one ever talked about. It happened in the 1930s during the Depression. She had become pregnant at 16 and had married the boy next door. Tragically, her first child died of TB before he was a year old. While pregnant with her second child, my mother's husband also contracted TB and was hospitalized out of town. She gave birth to her second baby who eventually also became ill from TB and died. My mother's husband never even knew the baby had passed before he himself succumbed to the disease. I cannot imagine having to deal with such tremendous loss and pain. Now I understood why she always wanted our family to stay together. As sad and painful as our home life was, it couldn't surpass the pain she had suffered as a teenager.

As I moved through the healing process, I realized that the wounding I received in my childhood had created an anger problem in me that came out mostly towards my husband and two sons. I had a terrible temper and often would overreact. It also led to drinking after work with coworkers, many times not even remembering how I got home. You can imagine this led to issues with my marriage and my children. So I went to my husband and to each of my sons asking for forgiveness for my fits of anger, for the ways I'd controlled them, and for any hurts I had caused them."

Eva's story is not uncommon. Many of us were acquainted with fear and pain growing up but have been unable to connect it to our current struggles. Have you ever had a physical wound that became worse over time? Looking back you realize you could have saved yourself a lot of trouble if you'd started with the proper treatment. That's how it is with what we are going to call "soul wounds." It wouldn't be too much to say that some of us would qualify as the "Walking Wounded"—people carrying everything from wounds of betrayal to abuse to broken hearts.

Soul wounds come in two primary forms: 1) traumatic life events and 2) painful human interactions.

1. Traumatic Life Events

You watch as your spouse slowly dies of cancer, your home is destroyed in a fire or storm, your brother commits suicide—all these cause trauma to the soul. Surviving a tornado, a near-drowning, a serious injury or illness, a car crash, violent war experiences, a kidnapping, rape or assault, having an abortion or pressuring a loved one to have one, childhood or spousal abuse, the untimely or tragic death of a family member, or even first-responder exposure to tragedy—the list could easily go on and on.

None of us likes pain. We humans are notorious for doing whatever it takes to avoid facing painful life experiences. Without even realizing it, we go into self-protective mode when exposed to severe or repeated trauma. We become experts at avoiding the full-impact of the painful experience. Some of us have stuffed our true feelings down so deeply that we have even become unaware of their existence.

An area that is often neglected is the process of *grieving our losses.* Many of us were taught to just "get on with life." Others of us have loved ones that are uncomfortable with our pain, so they may give us the impression that we should distract ourselves with busyness or new relationships. But grieving takes time. Grieving the loss of a spouse through death or divorce rarely takes less than two years. Grieving the loss of a child can take as many as ten years. But the loss of loved ones is not the only loss we need to grieve. We can need to grieve the loss of a dream, the loss of status, the loss of a job, or the loss of something we treasured. The scripture says that "hope deferred makes the heart sick." Some of us have pushed our heart-sickness down until we no longer recognize it.

2. Painful Human Interactions

To be human means to be vulnerable to the sins and weaknesses of others. If a person is to not just survive but thrive, he or she must get close to others and let them into the tender places of the heart.

Beginning with childhood, each of us is exposed daily to the potential of a wounded soul and sometimes even a broken heart. From cruel or shaming words to insults, betrayals, and broken promises, our hearts are fertile soil for rejection and pain.

In fact, rejection may just be the *single biggest source* of soul wounds. Some of us have experienced OVERT or obvious rejection. Perhaps we were abandoned emotionally or physically by one or both of our parents. We may have heard things like: "I wish you hadn't been born," or "you are nothing but a worthless piece of

> **To be human means to be vulnerable to the sins and weaknesses of others**

garbage." But most of us have been exposed to a much more subtle form of rejection called COVERT or hidden rejection.

Ten Examples of Covert Rejection:

- Death of a parent or significant person
- Divorce of parents
- Workaholic parent
- Addicted parent
- Absent parent (includes loving military parents)
- Critical parent
- Conditional love
- Comparison
- Over-protection
- Controlling or domineering parent

Barriers to Intimacy

Unhealed rejection can cause untold damage in our primary relationships. Without realizing what we're doing, we pass it on to those around us. That's because people who've been rejected erect barriers out of a desire for self-protection ("no one will ever hurt me like that again") or because we have tolerated the intolerable in our relationships (lack of healthy boundaries). We may even anticipate rejection where there is none or sabotage a healthy relationship with our fear of rejection.

In order to be the free and loving people God has called us to be, we must come out of hiding and move into healing. Rejection wounds *do not* heal themselves. Like all other soul wounds, they must be taken to God for healing.

God knows the depths of our emotional pain. He never tells us to fake it or push our pain down. Jesus mentioned this truth just before he endured his own time of intense suffering:

> *Here on earth you will have many trials and sorrows.*
> *But take heart, because I have overcome the world.*
> John 16:33

God also knows how easily we can be trapped into harboring resentment and bitterness. He gave us many warnings about neglecting the condition of our hearts:

> *Get rid of all bitterness, rage, anger, harsh words, and slander,*
> *as well as all types of evil behavior.*
> *Instead, be kind to each other, tenderhearted,*
> *forgiving one another, just as God through Christ has forgiven you.*
> Ephesians 4:31-32

In the face of all this, God boldly claims to be the Source of healing for all of our soul wounds:

> *He heals the brokenhearted and bandages their wounds.*
> Psalm 147:3

Three Essential Steps to Healing

Are you ready to find healing for your own soul wounds? If you are, you must stop pretending and lean *into* the pain. Here are the three essential steps you will need to take to find true relief:

1. Admit the truth of what happened without justifying or minimizing it.

We can't bring our pain to God if we keep denying it. He *invites* us to bring him our broken hearts. Begin by confessing to God and at least one other person the truth of what happened, even the things that seem small now but were huge to you as a child. Be sure to also admit any resulting resentment, bitterness, and judgment it caused. Since all people cannot necessarily be trusted, it's important to choose someone you know to be trustworthy.

And you will know the truth, and the truth will set you free.
John 8:32

*Confess your sins to each other and pray for each other
so that you may be healed.*
James 5:16

2. Forgive your offenders.

Remembering that forgiveness is an act of the will, not the emotions, intentionally choose now to forgive those who wounded you. Forgiving your offenders is the key that opens the door for *you* to go free. (See the chapter 7.0 Forgiveness for an in-depth understanding of the forgiveness process.) An amazing sense of peace awaits you!

*Be merciful, just as your Father is merciful.
Do not judge, and you will not be judged.
Do not condemn, and you will not be condemned.
Forgive and you will be forgiven.*
Luke 6:36-37

3. Ask God to heal your heart.

Give God permission to do whatever it takes to remove the wound (rejection, abandonment, etc.) and heal any leftover infection. Ask others to pray specifically for you to be healed. This is where the body of Christ is most vital. Sometimes we are too weak to even pray for ourselves or we don't know how to pray. The chapter 6.0 Permission addresses this more completely.

*The Lord is close to the broken-hearted and saves
those who are crushed in spirit.*
Psalm 34:18

DISCUSSION QUESTIONS:

1. To what traumatic events have you been subjected? List all you can remember:

2. Begin now to face the painful human interactions you have experienced, beginning with child-hood, then adolescence, and on through each decade of your life. Ask yourself, "Who has sinned against me in word or deed?" List here all the names of people or organizations that come to mind:

3. How has rejection impacted your life?

4. What are the soul wounds you have not fully faced and the losses you have not fully grieved? List them here:

4.6 A Distorted View of God

Everyone who knew Charlie loved him. Everyone, that is, except his own daughter, Mary Ann. Although she didn't know him, Mary Ann grew up hating her father. She hated the man she *thought* he was. Here's what happened:

> When she was four, Mary Ann's parents were divorced. Her mom Christine was a bitter woman who blamed Charlie for the divorce and began to poison Mary Ann's mind and heart with accusations against her dad. She refused Charlie all access to his daughter, secretly tossing all cards, letters and gifts into the trash. Mary Ann believed what she'd been told—that her father was a deadbeat dad who didn't even care enough to call her on her birthday.
>
> After many unsuccessful attempts to contact Mary Ann, Charlie's efforts grew further and further apart until finally he gave up. Twenty years passed. When Mary Ann was 34 years old, Charlie decided it was time to make one last desperate attempt to reach out to his daughter. Since previous calls had been met with rejection, Charlie knew he'd have to try a new tactic. So Charlie took on the identity of a distant uncle and called Mary Ann to say he was driving through town that week and would love to meet her for coffee. To his surprise and joy, Mary Ann said yes. Charlie and Mary Ann met that day and many more times over the next two years. Gradually, Mary Ann began to experience the genuinely loving nature of her father. Their relationship deepened. The day finally came when Charlie decided to risk it all by revealing his true identity. Choosing a nice restaurant for their meeting, Charlie prayed and then opened with these words: "I have a story to tell you." He told Mary Ann of a father who loved his daughter very much but had been forbidden to see or speak with her. After describing years of rejected calls, cards and gifts he ended by saying, "you are that little girl and I am your father."
>
> Mary Ann was overwhelmed. She had a lifetime of bitterness against an innocent father to release and a very difficult conversation ahead with her mother.

Under our CORE issues of pride, fear, unmet needs and unhealed wounds, there resides an even deeper issue. This deeper issue can cause a hard heart that won't allow healing in and can even *feed* the other core areas. This HARD CORE issue is a distorted view of God. No matter how it was formed, a distorted view of God will prevent his love from saturating our hearts. Just like Mary Ann, we can exist with walls that block and deny the truth of our Father's love. *Nothing* is more important because only the love of God can fully heal and restore us.

What can cause us to have a distorted view of God? Some of us grew up with parents who were unable to love us unconditionally. They may have been angry, depressed, addicted, selfish or simply absent but we learned to trust no one but ourselves. These feelings were easily transferred to God. If I'm not worthy of my own parents' love and attention, why would God want anything to do with me?

Others of us struggle with feelings of disappointment, resentment and even anger against God. We blame God for our pain or our losses. After all, God is all-powerful and could have stopped the event that caused our pain but didn't. We may never say it out loud, but we aren't sure if God really *is* good.

And then some of us were the victims of poor theology. We were taught what's called the "prosperity gospel"—that God exists to make our lives comfortable and pain-free. When things got tough or when we weren't healed, we blamed God.

If we are to grow emotionally and spiritually into all God wants for us as his children, we must honestly face the possibility of bitterness and distortion in our view of God Himself.

What we can know for sure about God? Here is a short list of characteristics the Bible gives us about God.

Nothing is more important because only the love of God can fully heal and restore us

A God Template

• Merciful	• Compassionate	• Gracious
• Slow to anger	• Abounding in love	• Forgiving
• Just	• Faithful	• Holy
• All-powerful	• All-knowing	• All-seeing

God is Both Loving and Righteous

God wanted his chosen servant Moses to see him clearly. He knew Moses had grown up as a 'throw away kid'—an adopted child coming from a disdained race. Moses had been exposed to the gods of Egypt. More than anything, Moses needed a better view of the one true God. So God the Father described himself with these words:

> *The LORD passed in front of Moses, calling out, "Yahweh" The*
> *LORD! The God of compassion and mercy! I am slow to anger and*
> *filled with unfailing love and faithfulness. I lavish unfailing love*
> *to a thousand generations. I forgive iniquity, rebellion, and sin.*
> *But I do not excuse the guilty. I lay the sins of the parents upon*
> *their children and grandchildren; the entire family is affected—even*
> *children in the third and fourth generations.*
> Exodus 34:6-7

Five Common God Distortions

1. Viewing God as an angry judge.

Some of us were taught that God would 'get us' if we misbehaved or sinned.

> *For no one is abandoned by the Lord forever. Though He brings*
> *grief, He also shows compassion because of the greatness of His*
> *unfailing love. For He does not enjoy hurting people*
> *or causing them sorrow.*
> Lamentations 3:31-33

2. Blaming God for our pain or for evil.

> *When tempted, no one should say, "God is tempting me." For God*
> *cannot be tempted by evil, nor does He tempt anyone.*
> James 1:13

3. Viewing God as impossible to please or as legalistically keeping score.

> *Lord, if you kept a record of our sins, who, O Lord, could ever*
> *survive? But you offer forgiveness, that we might learn to fear you.*
> Psalm 130:3-4

4. Pinning our parents' characteristics on God and rejecting Him for it.

During our formative years, our parents model God's character to us: loving, trustworthy, stable, and encouraging or absent, unreliable, harsh, critical, cold, and abusive. But what do the scriptures say?

> *Even if my father and mother abandon me,*
> *the Lord will hold me close.*
> Psalm 27:10

> *God is not a man, so He does not lie. He is not human, so He does*
> *not change His mind. Has He ever spoken and failed to act? Has He*
> *ever promised and not carried it through?*
> Numbers 23:19

> *"My thoughts are nothing like your thoughts," says the Lord. "And*
> *my ways are far beyond anything you could imagine. For just as*
> *the heavens are higher than the earth, so my ways are higher than*
> *your ways and my thoughts higher than your thoughts."*
> Isaiah 55:8-9

5. Seeing God as too small to handle our problems.

That's what Israel did. Time after time while delivering them from slavery in Egypt, God had done incredible miracles right before their eyes. But as soon as they heard about the size of the people living in the Promised Land, they forgot all that. They moaned and groaned and complained that they wanted to go back to the slavery of Egypt! God saw their hearts and knew they were really rejecting his power to save them. God rewarded the right heart attitude in a young man named Caleb.

> *But my servant Caleb has a different attitude than the others have.*
> *He has remained loyal to me, so I will bring him into the land he*
> *explored. His descendants will possess their full share of that land.*
> Numbers 14:24

A Love Barrier

If you've felt disappointment or resentment towards God, a thick wall of self-protection may have built up around your heart that keeps you from *experiencing* God's love. If so, you may have thoughts like to this: "I don't need God," "I can't risk being vulnerable," or "I'm afraid God might punish me." The truth is just the opposite. Led by the Holy Spirit, the Apostle Paul prayed this prayer that expresses the truth of God's love for you:

> *When I think of all this, I fall to my knees and pray to the Father,*
> *the Creator of everything in heaven and on earth. I pray that from*
> *his glorious, unlimited resources he will empower you with inner*
> *strength through his Spirit. Then Christ will make his home in*
> *your hearts as you trust in him. Your roots will grow down into*
> *God's love and keep you strong. And may you have the power to*
> *understand, as all God's people should, how wide, how long, how*
> *high, and how deep his love is. May you experience the love of*
> *Christ, though it is too great to understand fully. Then you*
> *will be made complete with all the fullness of life and power*
> *that comes from God.*
> Ephesians 3:14-19

Four Steps to Remove the Wall

The wall that keeps God's love at a distance *can* come down. But it won't happen unless you take specific action. If you are ready and willing to release all resentment and distortion in your view of God, take these four steps now:

1. **Confess it—admitting it exists is the beginning of its defeat.**

2. **Intentionally release all bitterness and judgment you've held against God.**

3. **Ask God to forgive you for blaming Him or for believing a lie about Him.**

4. **Ask God to do whatever it takes to tear down the wall and saturate your heart with His love!**

> *It is true that we live in the world,*
> *but we do not fight from worldly motives.*
> *The weapons we use in our fight are not the world's weapons*
> *but God's powerful weapons,*
> *which we use to destroy strongholds. We destroy false arguments;*
> *we pull down every proud obstacle that is*
> *raised against the knowledge of God;*
> *we take every thought captive and make it obey Christ.*
> 2 Corinthians 10:3-5 (GNT)

A Prayer to Release Judgment against God

Father, I confess that I have believed a lie—I have had a distorted and unfair image of you. You are holy and without sin and I have blamed you unfairly. I release all resentment, bitterness and unforgiveness against you now and I ask you to forgive me for judging you. Please forgive me for every way I have blamed you or believed a lie about you.

In the name of Jesus, I cancel Satan's authority over me in this area because I have chosen to repent and forgive. Holy Spirit, I give you permission to come into my heart and do whatever it takes to tear down the wall I've built around it. Father, I ask you saturate my heart with the knowledge and experience of your love.
In Jesus' name, Amen.

DISCUSSION QUESTIONS:

1. How do you see God? (Not how you think you *should* see God, but how you really feel deep inside.)

2. List the positive traits of your parents or primary caregivers:

3. List the negative traits of your primary caregivers:

4. Do you see any correlations between the characteristics of your caregivers and those you attribute to God?

5. Is there anything for which you have blamed God? Have you released all bitterness and judgment against him?

For further study:

Disappointment With God: Three Questions No One Asks Aloud by Philip Yancey

Totally Forgiving God: When It Seems He Has Betrayed You by R.T. Kendall

If God Is Good: Faith in the Midst of Suffering and Evil by Randy Alcorn

5.0 Confession

Principle Five: Confession

I find healing when I am willing to confess before God and another person the defects of character that he has revealed to me.

Make this your common practice: Confess your sins to each other and pray for each other so that you can live together whole and healed. The prayer of a person living right with God is something powerful to be reckoned with.
James 5:16

When our girls were about 8 and 10 years old, a 'crime' was committed during one of our frequent family get-togethers. My husband Ray and I were the proud owners of a fully loaded Olds 98. It wasn't new by any stretch of the imagination, but it was really nice—probably the nicest car we'd ever owned. While dinner was being prepared, we discovered that someone had scratched the words, "Tammy loves Billy" in the paint on the back of the car. Now it was obvious to the adults that the culprit had to be one or more of the younger kids. In our minds there were four possible suspects: our two girls and my sister's two boys, all between the ages of 8 and 10. We lined the four of them up and grilled them, using all kinds of parental pressure tactics to get the perpetrator(s) to confess. Nothing! No matter what we did, the kids continued to profess both their ignorance and innocence.

Fifteen years later, my younger daughter Arielle asked if I remembered the incident. I said, "Of course I remember—don't tell me you know who did it!" She looked shame-faced and admitted that she knew because *she* was the criminal! She'd been carrying that guilt for 15 years and finally couldn't stand it anymore!

What about you? Have you ever felt guilty but refused to confess what you'd done?

Brokenness can be the catalyst that initiates the breakdown of self-deception and pride. Although painful, it can be a *good* thing because it makes us much more likely to experience the benefits of CONFESSION.

We've spent the last several weeks doing an intentional truth search of our hearts. We've painstakingly examined the ways we've been offended and the ways we have offended others, always looking for roots of pride, fear, unmet needs, unhealed wounds, and a distorted view of God. To the best of our ability we've completed lists of those who've offended us as well as those we have offended. We know from experience that an honest look at our hearts often produces a painful season of brokenness and repentance.

The Four Benefits of Confession

The next step in our journey is to bring what we've discovered into the light of confession. Confessing our faults to God and to others brings multiple benefits. Let's look at four of the most important:

1. **Relief from guilt**

> *Finally, I confessed all my sins to you and stopped trying to hide*
> *my guilt. I said to myself, "I will confess my rebellion to the*
> *LORD." And you forgave me! All my guilt is gone.*
> Psalm 32:5

2. **Purity of heart**

> *If we confess our sins, He is faithful and just and will forgive us*
> *our sins and purity us from all unrighteousness.*
> 1 John 1:9

3. **Intimacy with God**

> *The Lord is close to the brokenhearted and*
> *saves those who are crushed in spirit.*
> Psalm 34:18

4. **Healing**

> *Therefore confess your sins to each other and pray for each other*
> *so that you may be healed. The prayer of a righteous person is*
> *powerful and effective.*
> James 5:16

I've seen the power of confession at work in many people, but perhaps never more dramatically than in a friend of mine I'll call Cathy. Cathy had kept a secret for many months before she and I sat down to talk. She told me that she'd been depressed and had suffered from severe insomnia. For the past two years, she had not even been able to sleep through one night. As we talked, Cathy gathered her courage and shared the incident she'd kept secret. We prayed and cried together and she left. The next morning, Cathy called me and told me that she'd slept all night long! Over the next months, she confirmed that her depression had lifted and she continued to be able to sleep well.

When we refuse to confess, the enemy of our souls is given a foothold in which to work. Darkness has a grip on that area of our lives. Confession breaks that darkness. Jesus' friend, John, didn't want us to miss this truth:

> *This is the message we heard from Jesus and now declare to you:*
> *God is light, and there is no darkness in Him at all. So we are lying*
> *if we say we have fellowship with God but go on living in spiritual*
> *darkness; we are not practicing the truth. But if we are living in*
> *the light, as God is in the light, then we have fellowship with each*
> *other and the blood of Jesus, His Son, cleanses us from all sin. If we*
> *claim we have no sin, we are only fooling ourselves and not living*
> *in the truth. But if we confess our sins to Him, He is faithful and*
> *just to forgive us our sins and to cleanse us from all wickedness.*
> 1 John 1:5-10

What Happens When We Don't Confess?

1. We become vulnerable to both physical and emotional disease.

> *When I refused to confess my sin, my body wasted away,*
> *and I groaned all day long.*
> Psalm 32:3

2. We feel distant from God.

> *If I had not confessed the sin in my heart,*
> *the Lord would not have listened.*
> Psalm 66:18

3. God's blessing is removed from our lives.

> *Whoever conceals their sins does not prosper,*
> *but the one who confesses and renounces them finds mercy.*
> Proverbs 28:13

The Process of Confession

Be intentional. Sit down with a trusted friend and read over both halves of your life inventory. You can then invite them to share feedback about any patterns they see, looking especially for the root issues we've discussed: fear, pride, unhealed wounds, unmet needs, and a distorted view of God. Keep these four suggestions in mind:

1. Choose a person you trust, someone you're sure will keep your confidences a secret. It is good select a person of the same gender who is not related to you. This will enable you to be completely free not to be concerned about their response to your revelations.

2. Choose a time when you won't be hurried. Planning for at least two hours is a good idea.

3. Choose a private place, one where you're sure you won't be interrupted.

4. Make a decision ahead of time to hold nothing back. It's the secrets of our lives that keep us locked in pain and dysfunction.

With God's help, we can take this important step. We can bring all the hidden junk of our lives out into the light of God's healing and love. We can be freed of guilt and begin to experience an even deeper intimacy with God. We *can* be healed! Begin practicing this principle with King David's beautiful prayer of confession:

A Prayer of Confession

Have mercy on me, O God, because of your unfailing love.
Because of your great compassion, blot out the stain of my sins.
Wash me clean from my guilt. Purify me from my sin.
For I recognize my rebellion; it haunts me day and night.
Against you, and you alone, have I sinned;
I have done what is evil in your sight.
You will be proved right in what you say,
and your judgment against me is just.
For I was born a sinner—
yes, from the moment my mother conceived me.
But you desire honesty from the womb,
teaching me wisdom even there.

Purify me from my sins, and I will be clean;
wash me, and I will be whiter than snow.
Oh, give me back my joy again;
you have broken me—now let me rejoice.
Don't keep looking at my sins. Remove the stain of my guilt.
Create in me a clean heart, O God. Renew a loyal spirit within me.
Do not banish me from your presence,
and don't take your Holy Spirit from me.

Restore to me the joy of your salvation,
and make me willing to obey you.
Then I will teach your ways to rebels, and they will return to you.
Forgive me for shedding blood, O God who saves;
then I will joyfully sing of your forgiveness.
Unseal my lips, O Lord, that my mouth may praise you.

You do not desire a sacrifice, or I would offer one.
You do not want a burnt offering.
The sacrifice you desire is a broken spirit.
You will not reject a broken and repentant heart, O God.
Psalm 51:1-17

DISCUSSION QUESTIONS:

1. Take a moment to read through the list below for patterns you've detected as you've faced your own junk. Check those with which you've struggled:

    ___ Addiction
    ___ Worry
    ___ Fear

___Anger/Rage
___Depression
___Bitterness/Resentment
___Anxiety
___Disrespect
___Greed
___Hypocrisy
___Self-deception
___Pride
___Sexual Immorality
___Dishonesty
___Lying
___Gossiping
___Other (list here)

2. Have you experienced a time of brokenness that propelled you into a deeper level of honesty and confession? Describe. How do you feel about that experience now?

3. Write out and share with your group a time when you experienced freedom, healing or renewed intimacy with God because you were willing to confess your faults both to God and to another person.

4. Are you ready to take the step of confession now? Who will you ask to listen to your confession? (List two or three people you are considering and begin praying now that God will direct you to the right one.)

6.0 Permission

Principle Six

I find healing when I stop trying to change myself and give God permission to do whatever it takes to change me.

Don't copy the behavior and customs of this world, but let God transform you into a new person by changing the way you think. Then you will learn to know God's will for you, which is good and pleasing and perfect.
Romans 12:2

In May of 2008, I woke up feeling fine. Around 4:30 that afternoon, I began to feel a painful tightening around my midsection. The feeling grew more and more uncomfortable until I could no longer bear to remain seated. By 6:00, I was on my way to the hospital in intense pain. After a long wait in the ER, tests revealed gallstones were causing the pain. Pain quickly changed my mind about the inconvenience of surgery.

I was referred to a surgeon with a great reputation. Dr. John Metersky had the exact skills I needed to fix my gall bladder problem. He was both willing and able. But until I gave him permission to operate, his skills did me no good.

Have you experienced a period of intense pain? Has that pain ever motivated you to deal with something you'd avoided before?

We've just finished looking back over our lives, getting honest and confessing all our junk to God and another person. Now we need to decide what to do about all we've faced. We have a choice. God could have designed us to function by instinct like other mammals. But He didn't. He makes it clear that His desire is that we avoid harmful ways, but God doesn't force us to follow His safety plan.

Three Things We Can Know about God's Will

1. God's desire is for our good.

God is for us. He's not a judge waiting to punish us, but a Father who wants to help and heal us.

"For I know the plans I have for you," says the Lord. "They are plans for good and not for disaster, to give you a future and a hope."
Jeremiah 29:11

God sent His Son into the world not to judge the world, but to save the world through Him.
John 3:17

2. God gives us the right to choose our own path.

God gives us control over our own individual choices:

> *"Today I have given you the choice between life and death, between*
> *blessings and curses. Now I call on heaven and earth to witness the*
> *choice you make. Oh, that you would choose life, so that you and*
> *your descendants might live!"*
> Deuteronomy 30:19

3. God waits to be invited to work in our lives.

We can resist the transformation process or we can submit to it. God gives us the choice. But God's will is for us to submit to Him and allow His wisdom to determine the areas and the timing of our healing.

> *Don't copy the behavior and customs of this world, but let God*
> *transform you into a new person by changing the way you think.*
> *Then you will learn to know God's will for you, which is good and*
> *pleasing and perfect.*
> Romans 12:2

Warning: Beware the Performance Trap!

We have just finished an intense truth search—including a potentially painful list of our negative tendencies. Our desire to change these tendencies could motivate us to slip into a do-it-yourself agenda. We may decide to 'white-knuckle' it because we want so badly to be different. This performance trap will set us up for failure every time.

Avoiding this temptation means recognizing the role *we* play and the role that God *alone* plays in the transformation of our souls.

- Only God can save us from the penalty of sin. This happens as God exchanges what we've earned (death) for what Christ earned (righteousness). Justification is a one-time act that occurs when we place our faith in Christ.

- Although only God can save us from the *power* of sin, we join him in the process of being saved from sin's power as we submit to the transformation of our souls. Our part in this is to get honest, to admit we need God's help, and to ask Him to change us. God then designs and brings about the needed change.

We can choose the self-help path (that's what most people do) or we can choose to give God permission to do whatever it takes to change us. I've tried it both ways. Each time I tried to fix myself, all I did was set myself up for failure. God is a more reliable and powerful source of healing. Will you invite Him to change you? If so, you may want to pray the Change Me, God Prayer:

The Change Me, God Prayer

Dear God, I see that there are things about my life that desperately need changing. I admit that my own attempts to change myself have failed. I come to you now giving you permission to do whatever it takes to change me into the person you desire me to be. I trust your promise that your plans for me are good and not evil. I place my faults, my habits, and my hurts in your hands. And I ask you to give me a nudge if I try to take them back.
In Jesus' name, Amen.

DISCUSSION QUESTIONS:

1. Have you ever thought about God's gift of free will in relation to your own process of transformation? How and when have you resisted that process?

2. Have you fallen into the Performance Trap (by trying to change yourself)? Describe a time when this happened.

3. What do you know for sure about God's will for you?

4. What fears come to mind as you think about giving God permission to do whatever it takes to change you?

7.0 Forgiveness

Principle Seven

I overcome by releasing all bitterness, resentment, and judgment toward everyone who has harmed me, yielding those areas to God alone.

God alone, who gave the law, is the Judge.
He alone has the power to save or to destroy.
So what right do you have to judge your neighbor?
James 4:12

Last week we admitted that we can't change ourselves. We gave God permission to do whatever it takes to change us. We may already be seeing differences in the ways we think, feel, and behave. Only God can change the human heart—that's His part! Now it's time to take responsibility for the things that only *we* can do something about—the unfinished business of our relationships. There are three areas in which we could have unfinished business: choosing to forgive, making amends, and setting appropriate boundaries. Let's begin with forgiving.

If you measured the times you've been deeply disappointed, wounded or betrayed in terms of bricks and stacked them one on top of another, how high would your stack be? My friend Betty has had to face a huge stack, probably about the size of the Empire State Building. Most of the bricks in her wall were caused by the murder of her then 21-year-old daughter Brenda. What makes the situation even more tragic is that this happened because of Brenda's attempt to prevent a young man's suicide. She had gone to a local University campus to share her 'God story' and was asked to remain afterward to talk. Brenda never came home. Her body was found strangled in the early hours of the morning.

From the first moment of shock to the annual parole hearings, Betty has faced a mountain of pain and grief. In all of this, she has repeatedly managed to move toward forgiving her daughter's murderer. As a result, Betty is amazingly free from the bitterness that could have eaten away at her soul.

You may not have faced a tragedy like Betty's, but chances are that you have your own stack of wounds and harms to forgive. Having just gone over an inventory of your life, you may see that stack more clearly now than ever before. We've just given our weaknesses, faults and hurts to God for healing. Now it's time to take responsibility for our part of cleaning up the mess of our lives. We do that by sorting through our life events and deciding who we need to forgive and then to whom we need to offer an apology and/or an amends. We'll begin first with the list of those we need to forgive.

Let's begin with a definition of what forgiveness is and what it is not:

Forgiveness is NOT:

➢ justifying the other person's behavior
➢ asking God to forgive them
➢ explaining away their behavior or understanding them
➢ forgetting what they did

> ➢ asking for their forgiveness
> ➢ denying that they have hurt you or sinned against you
> ➢ going to the person and telling them that you forgive them

Forgiveness is none of these things. According to Paul Thigpen, contributing editor for Discipleship Journal, there are two New Testament words translated "to forgive." Both mean "to let go" and "to cancel a debt." So forgiveness is simply this: an act of the will, done by faith, in which we give up our right to hold another person accountable for the wrong they have done us.

> **Forgiveness is an act of the will, done by faith, in which we give up our right to hold another person accountable for the wrong they have done us**

What Does the Bible Say About Forgiveness?

Forgiveness is a command of God that requires a voluntary act on our part:

> *Make allowance for each other's faults,*
> *and forgive anyone who offends you.*
> *Remember, the Lord forgave you, so you must forgive others.*
> Colossians 3:13

Forgiveness heals us, sometimes even physically. Take a look at the Five Health Benefits of Forgiveness:

The Five Health Benefits of Forgiveness

1. **Forgiveness lowers stress levels**
   According to a study done by Hope College researchers, one of the benefits of forgiveness is lower amounts of cortisol.

2. **Forgiveness keeps your heart healthy**
   One study suggests that people who hold on to grudges tend to have higher heart rates, while those who are more empathetic and able to forgive tend to have lower heart rates.

3. **Forgiveness lowers pain levels**
   Having a forgiving heart may lower both emotional and physical pain, according to a study done by Duke University Medical Center researchers. Out of 61 subjects who suffered from chronic back pain, those who were more likely to forgive reported lower levels of pain, leading researchers to believe that "a relationship appears to exist between forgiveness and important aspects of living with persistent pain."

4. **Forgiveness lowers blood pressure**

5. **Forgiveness extends life**

"The moment I start hating a man I become his slave. I can't enjoy my work anymore because he even controls my thoughts. My resentments produce too many stress hormones in my body and I become fatigued after only a few hours of work. The work I formerly enjoyed is now drudgery. Even vacations cease to give me pleasure. The man I hate hounds me wherever I go. I can't escape his tyrannical grasp on my mind…"
— S.I. McMillen, M.D., *None of These Diseases*

Refusing to Forgive Creates Distance from God

Jesus made a big deal of the importance of forgiving. He pointed out the unfairness of our unwillingness to forgive others when God has so generously forgiven us:

"But when you are praying, first forgive anyone you
are holding a grudge against, so that your Father in heaven
will forgive your sins, too."
Mark 11:25

For believers, does this mean we will be condemned to hell if we refuse to forgive? No. Jesus was talking about the distance in our relationship with God that is caused by our hard hearts. Pastor Brent Saathoff of CityChurch in San Antonio explains it this way:

"Forgiveness involves the release from guilt that comes from sin and bitterness. When we refuse to forgive others, God refuses to forgive us. In other words, we remain under the burden of guilt and bitterness until we forgive. This reality does NOT mean we go to hell. Our eternal destination is determined by our faith in His promise through Christ. You can be a child of God but still remain under the burden of unforgiveness, both yours towards others and God's towards you."
— Dr. Brent Saathoff

Our Refusal to Forgive Creates a Breeding Ground for the Kingdom of Darkness

Satan's forces gain a grip on us when we tolerate resentment, bitterness, and judgment toward others. In Matthew 18, Jesus used a parable (a word picture) to communicate the danger of accepting God's forgiveness while refusing to forgive our own offenders. He described a wise king who forgives his servant's huge debt then immediately discovers that servant's refusal to forgive his own offenders. Jesus ends the story with the king speaking these words:

'Shouldn't you have mercy on your fellow servant, just as I
had mercy on you?' Then the angry king sent the man to prison
to be tortured until he had paid his entire debt. "That's what
my heavenly Father will do to you if you refuse to forgive your
brothers and sisters from your heart."

The apostle John had heard these very words from Jesus and had taken them to heart. Years later he would counsel those under his leadership in a similar way:

> *If anyone claims, "I am living in the light," but hates a Christian*
> *brother or sister, that person is still living in darkness. Anyone*
> *who loves another brother or sister is living in the light and does*
> *not cause others to stumble. But anyone who hates another brother*
> *or sister is still living and walking in darkness. Such a person does*
> *not know the way to go, having been blinded by the darkness.*
> 1 John 2:9-11

A Special Warning about Bitterness

Chances are you have faced deep disappointment, have received wounds of rejection and betrayal, and have had unmet needs. Depending on your past, you responded as most of us do with a mixture of anger, resentment, pride, and fear. Here's the thing you need to know: bitterness will always follow when resentment is allowed to fester.

Bitterness will always follow when resentment is allowed to fester

God made us. He knows the many opportunities we've had for becoming wounded or rejected. And He knows our default is to store up resentment and bitterness. Listen to the warning of Hebrew 12:15:

> *Watch out that no poisonous root of bitterness*
> *grows up to trouble you, corrupting many.*

The bad news is that *bitterness is to the soul like cancer is to the body*—it will poison your thoughts and your emotions. Unrestrained, it will even affect your physical body, causing symptoms from headaches to digestive problems to autoimmune disorders. The good news is that there is a cure. *The cure for bitterness is forgiveness.* And God models the cure for us. We have rejected him, disappointed and grieved him deeply, yet he forgives us again and again. Jesus refused to allow himself to become bitter. He forgave while he walked the earth and he forgave an incomprehensible mountain of sin on the cross.

> *God forgave us all our sins; He canceled the unfavorable record of*
> *our debts with its binding rules and did away with it completely*
> *by nailing it to the cross.*
> Colossians 2:13-14

In what ways have you experienced rejection, betrayal, harm, or disappointment from others? Have you honestly faced the immensity of the wound you received? Have you applied the cure of forgiveness to the entire experience or have you minimized its effects with rationalizing thoughts like: "they didn't really mean it" or "other people have it much worse than I do"?

You can be free of all bitterness against others. As you make the choice to forgive, you will find that the person who'll go free is not your offender, but YOU! Jesus told us how to live without bitterness. He gave us the perfect tool to keep us free from its poison: He said, *"Pray like this:*

Our Father in heaven, may your name be kept holy. May your Kingdom come soon. May your will be done on earth as it is in heaven. Give us today the food we need, and forgive us our sins, as we have forgiven those who sin against us. And don't let us yield to temptation, but rescue us from the evil one. If you forgive those who sin against you, your heavenly Father will forgive you. But if you refuse to forgive others, your Father will not forgive your sins.
Matthew 6:9-15

We can't accept God's mercy and forgiveness without being willing to extend it to others. It won't work that way! If we want to live in grace, we must pass it on to the undeserving people around us.

Forgiveness is a Process

Forgiveness rarely begins with an emotion. It begins with an act of the will, a choice. Obedience to the command to forgive is possible in all cases, no matter how horrific the crime, because we are not commanded to *feel* forgiveness—we are commanded to *choose* it! Feelings will follow. They will. Remember Betty's story at the beginning of this chapter? Betty would never have avoided the trap of bitterness had she not persisted over years until her emotions lined up with her will. Forgiveness is a *process* that begins with a choice and ends when our feelings agree with that choice.

Our natural inclination is often to want to see our offender feel the pain they have inflicted on us or on those we love. We have a choice. We can fight that battle ourselves or we can give it to God and let him decide how to deal with the offender.

"When you lay down the burden of vengeance, God will pick it up."
— John Piper

In order to be free, you and I will need to thoroughly face the depth of the wounds we've received ourselves as well as those we've taken up an offense for on behalf of those we love. We will then need to make the forgiveness choice. No matter how deeply embedded a root of bitterness has become, we can eject that root with the choice to forgive. You have that power. It's your God-given right and command. Will you forgive?

When you are ready, pray the following prayer all the way through for each person on your list and *for each offense* you have held on to. (You could easily need to pray this 20-30 times over one person.) It is wise to make this declaration out loud because you are rejecting the forces of darkness that have had access to your soul because of your unforgiveness.

Remember—this is not about your *feelings*—it's an act of your *will*.

> **Forgiveness is a PROCESS that begins with a choice and ends when our feelings agree with that choice**

A Forgiveness Declaration

I choose to forgive _____ from my heart for
_____.

In the name of the Lord Jesus,
I cancel all their debts and obligations to me.
Heavenly Father, please forgive me for any bitterness,
hatred, or unforgiveness involved.
I ask you to forgive me for judging them.
In the name of Jesus and by the power of His blood,
I cancel Satan's authority over me in this area
because I have chosen to forgive.
Holy Spirit, I invite you into my heart and
ask you to heal me of all pain surrounding my wounds.
Please speak your words of truth to me about this situation.
In Jesus' name, Amen.

DISCUSSION QUESTIONS:

1. What does forgiveness mean to you?

2. To what extent have you struggled with forgiving others? With forgiving yourself?

3. What has prevented you from forgiving in the past?

4. How did your life change when you chose to forgive?

5. List here any person, group, or institution toward whom you've had feelings of resentment. Include those you have critical or judgmental thoughts about or those who've hurt someone you love.

6. Can you think of a situation in which you may have minimized how deeply you were wounded?

Recommended Reading:
The Art of Forgiving by Lewis Smedes
Total Forgiveness by R.T. Kendall

7.1 Inner Vows

My parents were children of the Great Depression of the 1930's. They learned to do without many necessities during their childhood and early adult years. They were taught never to waste *anything*. Mom scraped the inside of every jar of mayonnaise. She used bread wrappers instead of foil or plastic wrap to store leftovers. When I cut my leg on a piece of jagged metal, I wasn't taken to the doctor. Instead, my dad used his WWII medic skills to clean and close the three-inch cut on the back of my leg. I observed all of this and concluded, "When I grow up, I will *never* be cheap like my parents!"

Think back to your own childhood years. What messages did you receive that have programmed how you think and act today? Maybe you heard a lot of yelling and vowed never to get angry or maybe you watched your dad's drinking tear your family apart and decided never to marry a drinker. Chances are you *did* observe things you didn't like and formed judgments about what you saw. In this chapter, we are going to examine the power of what we are calling 'inner vows.'

What is an inner vow? An inner vow occurs when we decide that we are or are not going to do certain things based on a negative experience. Inner vows cause a subconscious mindset that determines what we are going to do in a given situation. Inner vows are often made out of a desire for self-preservation.

So if all I meant to do was to protect myself, why are they wrong? The wrongness of inner vows comes from the judgment we made against another person, gender, or group. Inner vows are harmful whether they are positive or negative because they put us in the place reserved for God alone. Listen to the words of Jesus:

> *"Do not judge others, and you will not be judged. For you will be*
> *treated as you treat others. The standard you use in judging is the*
> *standard by which you will be judged."*
> Matthew 7:1-2

Judgment is the sin issue at the core of all inner vows. Jesus knew that judging others would introduce darkness into our souls. He wanted to protect us from it. He knew that forgiveness is not complete as long as judgment remains. But that's not the only danger involved in making an inner vow. Paul taught that the person who *sows* judgment will always *reap* judgment:

> *Do not be deceived: God cannot be mocked.*
> *A man reaps what he sows.*
> Galatians 6:7 (NIV)

Add to that the warning of Jesus to avoid vow-making all together:

> *"You have also heard that our ancestors were told, 'You must not*
> *break your vows; you must carry out the vows you make to the*
> *Lord.' But I say, do not make any vows! Do not say 'By heaven!'*
> *because heaven is God's throne. And do not say, 'By the earth!'*
> *because the earth is His footstool. And do not say, 'By Jerusalem!'*
> *for Jerusalem is the city of the great King. Do not even say, 'By my*

head!' for you can't turn one hair white or black.
Just say a simple, 'Yes, I will,' or 'No, I won't.'
Anything beyond this is from the evil one.
Matthew 5:33-37

Inner Vows and Our Emotions

Humanity's fall into sin affected all of us in at least four ways: spiritually, mentally, emotionally, and physically. When dealing with emotions, most of us tend to fall into one of two extremes: either we repress our feelings or we allow our feelings to run our lives. We need the help of the Holy Spirit to get free of all destructive messages and judgments. As we become more honest about our subconscious or repressed emotions, our relationships will improve. Examining our childhood messages and any resulting inner vows can help. We will begin this process using the following checklist.

A Checklist of Common Inner Vows

List all the vows you have ever made. Begin by reviewing this list of common inner vows. Continue by adding any others you have made:

___I will never be like my father/mother (underline which)
___I will never discipline my kids the way I was disciplined
___I will never treat my kids the way my parents treated me
___I will never desert my kids
___I will never get married (or get married again)
___I will never let anyone hurt me again
___I will never marry anyone like my mother/father (underline which)
___I will never go to work and leave my kids at home
___I am going to make sure my kids get the things or opportunities I didn't get
___No one is going to tell me what to do/say/eat
___No one is going to control me
___No woman will ever control me like my mom did my dad
___No man will control me like my dad did with my mom
___I will never trust another man/woman (underline which)
___I will never let anyone else take advantage of me
___I will never work for another man/woman (underline which)
___I will never do business with another Christian
___I will never trust another pastor
___I will never treat my spouse the way my father did my mother
___I will never scream at my kids like my mom did
___I will never go to church again
___I will never work for anyone else again
___I will never be free/well
___I will never lose weight/quit smoking/quit drinking/etc.
___I will never let my kids go through what I went through
___My kids will all have a college education

___I'd kill anyone who hurt my kids
___I can do it by myself
___Other _____
_____
_____

As we continue to choose healing and freedom, we will notice improvement in our relationships, both with God and with others. Removing Inner Vows is one more step in that process.

A Prayer to Cancel Inner Vows

Father, I confess that I have vowed _____.
I choose now to forgive those I have judged. I ask you to forgive
me for putting myself in your place by judging them. I release this
area to you now—please take control and purify it. I ask that you
reverse the consequences of this vow. In Jesus' name, Amen.

A Prayer to Complete the Process

Father, I want to be free of all the resentment and judgment I've
gathered over the years. I invite you to make me aware of any other
unconscious judgments I've made. I trust you to continue to show
me these things until I am completely free. In Jesus' name, Amen.

DISCUSSION QUESTIONS:

1. What are some of the messages (spoken or unspoken) that you received in childhood?

2. How have these messages affected your behavior as an adult?

3. Are you more likely to repress/deny your emotions or to live by them?

4. List the inner vows you've detected here:

7.2 Healthy Boundaries

A few years ago I met John Townsend, author of the national best-seller *Boundaries*, at a conference by the same name. John explained that when facing the pressure of a 'boundary-buster,' none of us owes that person an explanation, much less a list of excuses, of why we aren't able to comply with his/her wishes. A simple "I'm just not able to do that right now" is sufficient and builds respect. John explained that anything else gives the boundary-buster the very ammunition he or she needs to poke holes in our list and to talk us into giving in to his/her will. I knew I needed John's advice, so I memorized the words, "I'm just not able to do that right now." Little did I know I was going to need them the very next day....

Sure enough, the next morning I found myself confronted by my personal boundary-buster. He met me in the church hallway and imperiously asked, "Why aren't you in the leaders' class? ALL my leaders are in that class!" I felt myself begin to panic until I remembered my new mantra. I looked directly into his eyes and calmly stated, "I'm just not able to do that right now." To my amazement, the Boundary-Buster responded by pulling back a little and gazing at me with new respect while answering, "Oh, okay." As he turned and walked away, I felt a rush of empowerment and freedom! Why hadn't I done that a long time ago?

Have you ever faced (or lived with) a boundary buster? If so, you may be ready to take this next step of building healthy boundaries. We've listed those we've offended and made amends to the best of our ability. And we've listed those who've offended *us* and have chosen to forgive them. But what if some of those people are still making bad choices that are impacting us today? How do we prevent ourselves from going back to a place of resentment?

Setting Healthy Boundaries

The answer is found in learning what it means to set healthy boundaries. Perhaps you've heard the Robert Frost quote, "Good fences make good neighbors." Like fences, boundaries separate my responsibilities from yours. People with healthy boundaries do three things: they accept personal responsibility, they say no when appropriate, and they humbly refuse to tolerate disrespect.

God Has Healthy Boundaries

Are boundaries really necessary? Is this some modern psychological technique? Actually, the whole idea of boundaries comes from God himself. God is both just and loving. He doesn't control us—he lets us make our own choices. But he does let us know that our disobedience produces consequences.

> *Do not be deceived: God cannot be mocked.*
> *A man reaps what he sows.*
> Galatians 6:7

A Strategy for Dealing with Three Categories of People

God deals with people according to their behaviors and choices—maybe we should consider doing the same. The Old Testament book of Proverbs is considered the book of wisdom. It contains the sayings of King Solomon, the wisest man on earth. Solomon divided people into three categories and directed his listeners to adapt their responses based on the type involved. The categories he mentions are these: wise people, foolish people, and evil people.

1. Wise People

When dealing with a wise person, it's safe to use words because they are humble enough to listen and to consider change. You can recognize a wise person because they are open to feedback, take responsibility for their problems, and show remorse when they find they've hurt others.

> *So don't bother correcting mockers; they will only hate you.*
> *But correct the wise, and they will love you.*
> *Instruct the wise, and they will be even wiser.*
> *Teach the righteous, and they will learn even more.*
> *Proverbs 9:8-10*

2. Foolish People

Foolish people are defensive, make excuses to avoid taking responsibility, and respond to truth with anger, disdain, or an "I'm all bad" stance. They have little awareness of the frustration they cause others. They see themselves as the victim, always looking for someone who will rescue and agree with them. Save yourself some time and frustration—don't waste your breath when dealing with a foolish person! Set limits on what you will tolerate and, when appropriate, use consequences that cause them to feel the pain of their irresponsible choice. What advice does God give us for interacting with foolish people?

> *Don't answer the foolish arguments of fools,*
> *or you will become as foolish as they are.*
> Proverbs 26:4

> *If a wise man has an argument with a fool,*
> *the fool only rages and laughs, and there is no quiet.*
> Proverbs 29:9

3. Evil People

There is only one response to evil people: do *whatever it takes* to avoid them or escape from them completely. These are the rare folks who actually enjoy hurting others—they can be recognized by the presence of three characteristics:
- they have a façade of respectability
- they will never admit they're wrong
- people around them are suffering and sometimes even dying

God's advice to us concerning evil people is clear:

> *Evil people only want to harm others.*
> *Their neighbors get no mercy from them.*
> Proverbs 21:10

> *Anyone who corrects the wicked will get hurt.*
> Proverbs 9:7

Codependency: Disease of the Good Guys

Some of us have lived all of our lives without healthy boundaries. We have difficulty saying no, we form one-sided or destructive relationships, and we take more than our share of responsibility. Is this merely a coincidence or is there something else going on here—something predictable? Let's look at what it takes to grow up to be emotionally healthy.

As we discussed in the chapter on Unmet Needs, every human being comes into this world with basic *emotional* as well as physical needs—needs for love, affection, attention, comfort, encouragement, belonging, approval, respect, security, etc. We can *survive*, but we *won't thrive* when we do without them for any significant period of time. The result is a condition called codependency. (It can also be called relationship addiction.) Codependency most often occurs when you have lived with an emotionally unavailable person—someone who, due to depression or addiction or selfishness or absence, did not *voluntarily* meet your basic emotional needs.

> **Codependency most often occurs when you've lived with an emotionally unavailable person**

Codependents frequently experience:

- Physical ailments
- Workaholism
- Denial and repression
- Guilt for everything that happens to everyone around them
- Depression and loneliness
- Resentment and anger
- Anxiety

> "Codependency is a compulsion to control and rescue people by fixing their problems. It occurs when a person's God-given needs for love and security have been blocked in a relationship with a dysfunctional person, resulting in a lack of objectivity, a warped sense of responsibility, being controlled and controlling others (three primary characteristics); and in hurt and anger, guilt, and loneliness (three corollary characteristics)."
> — Pat Springle, *Overcoming Codependency*

This pattern is recognized by certain common features: the codependent is attracted to people who are irresponsible and need to be rescued or 'fixed.' They then expend large amounts of energy trying to get the one they care about to do the right thing. You know this is you when you spend more time thinking about how to solve your loved one's problems than *they* do! Even worse, your superhuman efforts are most likely unappreciated and unsuccessful, leaving you holding a big bag of resentment. There are three common characteristics of codependents:

- Low self-esteem
- Poor personal boundaries
- Anger/guilt over the choices of others

Healing of codependency occurs as we search out and seek healing for the core issues that feed it. Look especially for unmet needs, but also explore unhealed wounds, fear, pride, and a distorted view of God.

Your Part

Rare is the person who automatically holds up strong healthy boundaries both internally and externally. No matter your background, you *can* make this choice. But you must be intentional. You can sort through the list of those that have harmed you and decide if a new, stronger boundary is necessary to prevent you from falling back into your old pattern of resentment. Saying 'no' may be the best thing you can do right now to move into healthier living.

Keep in mind that your goal is to allow the consequences (and sometimes pain) for the choices of the irresponsible or selfish people in your life to move from *your* shoulders to *theirs*. For instance, if your adult child is irresponsible with money and then can't make their car payment, you do not step in to rescue them. You say, "I'm sorry to hear that" and then stop talking. If your spouse is verbally abusive, you might say, "I hope that you will not use name-calling in the future but if you do, I want you to know that I will be leaving the room." The goal is to allow the natural consequences of your loved one's choice to fall on them. Painful consequences are often the *only* effective motivator for life change.

What if someone close to you is going through an unusually hard time? Is it okay to come to their rescue? Absolutely! The Apostle Paul gave clear instructions for when we should and should not step in to help carry the load of those around us:

> ***Share each other's burdens*** [a temporary overburden],
> ***and in this way obey the law of Christ.***
> Galatians 6:2

But…

> ***Each one should test their own actions. Then they can take pride in***
> ***themselves alone, without comparing themselves to someone else,***
> ***for each one should carry their own load*** [a light knapsack].
> Galatians 6:4-5

Verse 2 tells us to share the temporary overburdens of our friends and family, while verse 5 tells us that each person should carry his own daily responsibility. (Temporary overburdens are things that are not a consequence of their irresponsibility, like a battle with cancer or the loss of a family member).

We can choose to go on tolerating intolerable behavior or we can follow the example of God the Father and establish healthier boundaries for ourselves and for those with whom we regularly come in contact. We can hold up the bar of respect and become peace*makers* instead of just peace-*keepers*! Here's a great prayer to help us follow through on our boundaries:

The Serenity Prayer

God, grant me the serenity
To accept the things I cannot change,
The courage to change the things I can,
And the wisdom to know the difference.
Living one day at time;
Enjoying one moment at a time;
Accepting hardship as a pathway to peace;
Taking, as Jesus did,
This sinful world as it is,
Not as I would have it;
Trusting that You will make all things right
If I surrender to Your will,
So that I may be reasonably happy in this life,
And supremely happy with You forever in the next.
Amen.

DISCUSSION QUESTIONS:

1. Have you ever lived with or been in a close relationship with a boundary buster (someone who used guilt or power or anger to control you)? How did this person's choices affect your life?

2. Are there people in your life that fit the category of wise people? List the ones who come to mind here:

3. Are there people in your life that fit the category of foolish people? List them here:

4. Do you currently know or have you ever known an evil person?

5. Do you see any of the traits of codependency in yourself? List them here:

6. What relationships do you currently have that need better boundaries?

8.0 Amends

Principle Eight

I overcome by taking responsibility for the harm I've caused by my words or actions, asking forgiveness whenever possible.

Fools mock at making amends for sin,
but goodwill is found among the upright.
Proverbs 14:9

In the 70's, I received a bachelor's degree in Sociology and began my professional career as a Children's Protective Services Social Worker for the state of Florida. Seeing some distressing abusive situations, I remember thinking, "I would NEVER hit a child." I thought then as I do now that slapping a child in the face is totally unacceptable. Needless to say, I was both shocked and horrified a few years later when I violated my own rule. After a particularly heated interchange with my 13 year-old daughter, I slapped her cheek. Both of us were shocked and upset, retreating to our separate rooms in tears. A few minutes later, I knew what I had to do. I found Aimee Beth and immediately wrapped my arms around her, telling her that what I did was totally wrong and asking for her forgiveness. I'm still amazed and grateful at how instantly and completely she gave it to me.

Maybe you haven't been guilty of slapping someone in the face, but odds are you *have* injured someone by your words, actions, or attitude. Have you been able to seek forgiveness from each of them? Your own healing and freedom could easily hang on following through with this principle.

Making Amends

In the "MY PART" column of our inventory sheets, we listed our choices or responses that wounded others or offended God. Now it's time to right our wrongs as best we can. We do this by making amends for the harm we've caused by our words, actions, or attitudes, being careful to ensure that we cause no further harm to those involved.

Foolish people laugh at making things right when they sin.
But honest people try to do the right thing.
Proverbs 14:9

Although we can't undo what's been done in the past, we can express sincere regret for the pain we've caused and can make a commitment not to repeat our past mistakes. Through Moses, God instructed the people of Israel to intentionally make amends. He said,

"Give the following instructions to the people of Israel: if any
of the people—men or women—betray the Lord by doing wrong
to another person, they are guilty. They must confess their sin
and make full restitution for what they have done, adding an
additional 20 percent and returning it to the person who was

> *wronged. But if the person who was wronged is dead, and there are*
> *no near relatives to whom restitution can be made, the payment*
> *belongs to the Lord and must be given to the priest. Those who are*
> *guilty must also bring a ram as a sacrifice, and they will be purified*
> *and made right with the Lord. All the sacred offerings that the*
> *Israelites bring to a priest will belong to him. Each priest may keep*
> *all the sacred donations that he receives."*
> Numbers 5:6-10

This is especially good news for pastors! Seriously, though, this principle is as important for us as it was for the Israelites. It is often the "next right thing" for us. Jesus thought so. He even made making amends a higher priority than public worship:

> *"You have heard that our ancestors were told, 'You must not*
> *murder. If you commit murder, you are subject to judgment.'*
> *But I say, if you are even angry with someone, you are subject to*
> *judgment! If you call someone an idiot, you are in danger of being*
> *brought before the court. And if you curse someone, you are in*
> *danger of the fires of hell. So if you are presenting a sacrifice*
> *at the altar in the Temple and you suddenly remember that someone*
> *has something against you, leave your sacrifice there*
> *at the altar. Go and be reconciled to that person. Then*
> *come and offer your sacrifice to God."*
> Matthew 5:21-24

There are many ways to make amends, ranging from offering simple apologies to making monetary restitution. Amends can be made in person, by phone, or in writing. The most direct method is usually the best. The seven most powerful words to use when making amends are these: "I was wrong—will you forgive me?"

Saying "I'm sorry" is cheap. It costs you very little and it doesn't allow you to own responsibility for your actions. It also doesn't call for a response from the one you've offended. The best amends happen when we sincerely say "I was wrong—will you forgive me?" and then stop talking. Allow the other person time to respond.

A word of caution is needed here. Since human relationships involve two imperfect people, it can be tempting to use this as an opportunity to point out our friend's faults. This is especially true when we believe our friend has harmed us even more than we've harmed them! We are called to resist this temptation, remembering that we are not here to pluck the speck out of our friend's eye, but to deal with the log in our own. Jesus warned us about this temptation:

Use the seven most powerful words: "I was wrong—will you forgive me?"

> *"And why worry about the speck in your friend's eye when you*
> *have a log in our own? How can you think of saying to your friend,*
> *'Let me help you get rid of that speck in your eye,' when you can't*
> *see past the log in your own eye? Hypocrite! First get rid of the log*

*in your own eye; then you will see well enough to deal
with the speck in your friend's eye."*
Matthew 5:3-5

Using the word "but" in any context in your apology invalidates everything else you've said and allows you to shift blame away from yourself.

For example: "Lizzie, I regret the critical way I responded to you when you were a teenager **but** I wouldn't have done that if you hadn't been so disrespectful!"

The Apostle Paul had a suggestion for someone desiring to make amends for stealing: *"If you are a thief, quit stealing. Instead, use your hands for good hard work, and then give generously to others in need"* (Ephesians 4:28). Jesus affirmed a notorious tax collector and thief named Zacchaeus for making the decision to make amends:

*Zacchaeus stood before the Lord and said, "I will give half my
death to the poor, Lord, and if I have cheated people of their
taxes, I will give them back four times as much!" Jesus responded,
"Salvation has come to this home today, for this man has shown
himself to be a true son of Abraham."*
Luke 19:8-9

It can be helpful to ask for the advice of a trusted friend in choosing the form of amends you will make in each case, especially in situations in which bringing up the past might reopen old wounds and make matters worse. Remember Jesus' counsel to us in Matthew 7:12: "Treat others as you want them to treat you." In some cases, direct amends may not be appropriate. There are situations that might be further harmed by direct or even indirect contact. In these cases, or when the person involved is missing or dead, it's possible to write a heartfelt letter of amends and read it to a trusted friend before destroying it. Or you might choose to invest your time and energy in others who are in similar situations to the one you harmed.

> **Using the word "but" in any context in your apology invalidates everything else you've said**

It's important to note that some of us have long been carrying a warped sense of responsibility. We have blamed ourselves for everything bad that happened to anyone close to us. We've believed ourselves to be the source of pain and suffering in our own lives and in the lives of those around us.

Others of us have focused so long on how others have failed us, that we haven't spent the time needed to honestly access our own responses and choices! Honestly working through this principle will provide the opportunity to learn the difference between what is and isn't our responsibility. It will help us take a more realistic look at the effects of our actions.

It is not unusual to discover that the person we've damaged the most is ourselves! We've had unrealistic expectations for ourselves, refusing to admit that we are only human. This can mean neglecting the needs of our bodies, our souls, and our spirits. We have lived with what author and physician, Richard Swenson, calls a lack of margin. Dr. Swenson refers to margin as the space between ourselves and our limitations. Some of us are exhausted and stressed as a normal way of existence. He diagnoses many of us living in the 21st century with these words:

"Something's wrong. People are tired and frazzled. People are anxious and depressed. People don't have the time to heal anymore. There is a psychic instability in our day that prevents peace from implanting itself very firmly in the human spirit."
— Richard Swenson, M.D., *Margin*

Living on the edge impacts us in four primary ways: emotional energy, physical energy, time, and finances. Perhaps we need to put our own name at the top of our amends list! How can you begin now to stop repeating the mistakes of the past that have brought you harm or distress?

Since the beginning, humans have been good at blaming and poor at taking responsibility for their choices. You can be different. You can be the one of the few that follows the path God has laid out by intentionally owning your choices and by making right your wrongs.

The Amends Process

- Make a list of those you have harmed from column 5 of your Harms Inventory list (those to whom you owe an amends).

- Next to each name, write your plan for making specific amends.

- Review your plans with a trusted friend and make changes as appropriate.

- Begin making amends, placing a check mark next to each plan as you complete it.

We can expect to experience relief from a weight of guilt as we faithfully work through each of our amends. Our sense of peace will increase. Our joy will grow. God delights to pour out blessings on our efforts of obedience and humility.

A Prayer before Making Amends

God, I want to obey you in making right
every wrong you've shown me.
You know the situations that are heavy on my heart.
You know those I should contact and
those where further harm would occur if I did.
I need your wisdom to guide me.
Keep me honest and give me the courage to take
responsibility for my part only.
In Jesus' name, Amen.

DISCUSSION QUESTIONS:

1. When you are wrong, how difficult is it for you to admit it and to sincerely apologize?

2. What makes this especially difficult for you?

3. Make a list of those you've harmed and what you did. List them here:

   A. Is there anyone you've borrowed money from and have not repaid?
      (Include family, friends, and businesses.) List name and amount owed:

   B. Have you stolen from anyone, including office supplies from a workplace?
      List them and the item(s) you stole here:

   C. Have you broken a promise to anyone? List:

D. To whom have you lied? List:

E. All others:

4. Is there anyone you are unwilling to face and admit your wrongs? Why? (It is wise to discuss difficult situations with a pastor or trusted friend before approaching them.)

9.0 Authority

Principle Nine

I overcome by using the authority that Christ has given me to resist evil, refusing to tolerate darkness in my own heart.

Submit yourselves therefore to God.
Resist the devil, and he will flee from you.
James 4:7

Debra lived with nicotine addiction for years. She tried to quit many times. Sometimes she'd stop for a few days, sometimes even for a few months. But no matter how hard she tried, Debra never lost the desire for a cigarette and never could stay free. Although she had been through our church's recovery process and had even served as a leader, Debra still was stuck in her addiction. But everything changed on July 28, 2008. That's the day Debra decided she would never be able to effectively minister to others while addicted. She had heard that generational patterns are sometimes handed down from our parents and grandparents, attaching to us in the form of spiritual bondage. Debra suspected this was the case with her family.

That day Debra asked for prayer to set her free from nicotine addiction. We prayed, using the name of Jesus to take authority over every enemy of the cross that was taking advantage of her, especially those working in the area of nicotine addiction. God answered our prayer and Debra went home free! She no longer even wanted a cigarette. Debra continues to be completely free today.

Do you know someone who has tried everything they know to stop a destructive habit or to break a pattern of fear, lust or rage? Maybe that someone is you. If you feel stuck, working through this principle might be just what you need to open a door of freedom.

Two Definitions

We live in a world that consists of two very real but invisible kingdoms: the kingdom of God and the kingdom of darkness. Let's look at a definition for each:

1. The Kingdom of God

The kingdom of God is made up of every being, whether angelic or human, that submits to the authority of God.

For he has rescued us from the dominion of darkness
and brought us into the kingdom of the Son he loves,
in whom we have redemption, the forgiveness of sins.
Colossians 1:13-14

We know that God's children do not make a practice of sinning,
for God's Son holds them securely, and the evil one cannot touch

> *them. We know that we are children of God*
> *and that the world around us is under the control of the evil one.*
> 1 John 5:18-19

2. The Kingdom of Darkness

The kingdom of darkness is made up of every being, whether demonic or human, that resists or rebels against the authority of God.

> *Once you were dead because of your disobedience and your many*
> *sins. You used to live in sin, just like the rest of the world, obeying*
> *the devil—the commander of the powers in the unseen world. He*
> *is the spirit at work in the hearts of those who refuse to obey God.*
> *All of us used to live that way, following the passionate desires*
> *and inclinations of our sinful nature. By our very nature we were*
> *subject to God's anger, just like everyone else.*
> Ephesians 2:1-3

Understanding Our Enemy's Schemes

Scripture teaches that Satan leads the forces of darkness in intentional schemes against the people of God, both as individuals and as a group. The desire of our enemy is to make us either *ignorant* of its existence or *intimidated* by it! It's obvious that many in our culture think of Satan as a make-believe character with a red suit and a pitchfork. This is okay with our enemy because our ignorance allows them to go undetected and unchallenged.

If ignorance doesn't work, Satan's forces move to their second tactic, intimidation. Satan is not too concerned if a believer is awakened to the truth of his existence as long as he can keep that believer in fear or at least unable to use his God-given authority to resist and evict his minions. But God desires that we open our eyes to the reality of darkness while accepting and using the authority Jesus passed on to us to evict them from our lives.

> *So humble yourselves before God.*
> *Resist the devil, and he will flee from you.*
> James 4:7

How the Enemy Gains Access

There are three primary doors through which the enemy of our souls gains access:

1. Our Own Sinful Choices

The kingdom of darkness can't function in the light. Sin gives the kingdom of darkness power over us because we are functioning in *its* territory.

> *When you follow the desires of your sinful nature, the results are*
> *very clear: sexual immorality, impurity, lustful pleasures, idolatry,*
> *sorcery, hostility, quarreling, jealousy, outbursts of anger, selfish*

ambition, dissension, division, envy, drunkenness,
wild parties, and other sins like these.
Galatians 5:19-21

Even as children of God, we can yield ourselves to further either kingdom:

Anyone who claims to live in God's light and hates a brother or
sister is still in the dark. It's the person who loves brother and
sister who dwells in God's light and doesn't block the light from
others. But whoever hates is still in the dark, stumbles around in
the dark, doesn't know which end is up, blinded by the darkness.
1 John 2:9-11

"Do not judge others, and you will not be judged.
Do not condemn others, or it will all come back against you.
Forgive others, and you will be forgiven."
Luke 6:37

2. The Sinful Choices of Others

We need to know that we are *not* held responsible for the sins others have committed against us:

The child will not be punished for the parent's sins, and the parent
will not be punished for the child's sins.
Ezekiel 18:20

But we *are* held responsible for our sinful responses to what happened. The failure to forgive creates distance between us and our heavenly Father and creates fertile soil for the enemy. (Don't forget—sometimes the person you most need to forgive is *yourself!*)

"If you forgive those who sin against you, your heavenly
Father will forgive you. But if you refuse to forgive others,
your Father will not forgive your sins."
Matthew 6:14-15

Jesus clashed most with religious people who were full of judgment and self-righteousness. He called them "sons of vipers"! If we want to avoid the pitfall of Jesus' enemies, we must create a zero tolerance zone in our hearts for the sins of judgment and unforgiveness.

Unfortunately, gross sin defiles everyone involved in it, even the innocent. Picture yourself standing on the edge of a pigpen—one filled with mud, rotted food, urine and even feces. Whether you jumped into that pigpen voluntarily or someone came up and pushed you in, you would still be covered with filth. In much the same way, defilement spreads to the innocent victim of another person's sinful choice. (Children who've been molested often feel shame even though they had no choice in what happened.)

3. Generational Patterns

God has every reason to wipe us out but allows his mercy to override his justice. He limits the natural fallout of our sinful choices to the third and fourth generation only.

> *You must not bow down to them or worship them, for I, the Lord your God, am a jealous God who will not tolerate your affection for any other gods. I lay the sins of the parents upon their children; the entire family is affected—even children in the third and fourth generations of those who reject me. But I lavish unfailing love for a thousand generations on those who love me and obey my commands.*
>
> Exodus 20:5-6

Social scientists confirm that negative patterns are passed down from generation to generation. The enemy targets us where we are already weakest. Whether it is alcohol, food addiction, anger, sexual immorality or legalism, what begins with one generation often gains momentum in subsequent ones. Sinful patterns are inherited unless we face our propensities and seek freedom from their bondage in Christ.

One way we can find increase the light and freedom our family lives in is when we repent for and renounce the sins of our ancestors. That's what Old Testament prophet Daniel did. Daniel was one of the few Biblical heroes with no record of bad choices or attitudes. Yet he got on his knees and cried out to God for forgiveness, including himself in the sins of his people:

> *During the first year of his reign, I, Daniel, learned from reading the word of the Lord, as revealed to Jeremiah the prophet, that Jerusalem must lie desolate for seventy years. So I turned to the Lord God and pleaded with him in prayer and fasting.... I prayed to the Lord my God and confessed: "O Lord, you are a great and awesome God! You always fulfill your covenant and keep your promises of unfailing love to those who love you and obey your commands. But we have sinned and done wrong. We have rebelled against you and scorned your commands and regulations. We have refused to listen to your servants the prophets, who spoke on your authority to our kings and princes and ancestors and to all the people of the land....O my God, lean down and listen to me. Open your eyes and see our despair. See how your city—the city that bears your name—lies in ruins. We make this plea, not because we deserve help, but because of your mercy. "O Lord, hear. O Lord, forgive. O Lord, listen and act! For your own sake, do not delay, O my God, for your people and your city bear your name."*
>
> Daniel 9:2-6, 18-19

What is a Stronghold?

In Bible times, everyone knew that a physical stronghold was a fortified place, similar to a modern fort. A spiritual stronghold is an area of spiritual bondage created by repetitive sin. It means being 'stuck' or unable to choose by a simple act of the will to break out of a destructive habit, emotion, or thought pattern. Think of the predicament of a person who is stuck in quicksand. The more he struggles, the further down he goes. He needs someone on solid ground to throw him a rope and pull him out! In the same way, God never meant for any of us to fight alone. The body of Christ is designed to build us up, comfort us, and help us when we are overwhelmed.

The weapons we fight with are not the weapons of the world.
On the contrary, they have divine power to demolish strongholds.
We demolish arguments and every pretension that sets itself up
against the knowledge of God, and we take captive every thought
to make it obedient to Christ.
2 Corinthians 10:4-5

How Are Believers Targeted?

The Bible uses the term "demonized" to describe the attachment of demonic spirits to those Jesus and the disciples ministered to in Israel. There are three levels of demonic attack against believers:

1. **Harassment** (This includes all forms of deception, accusation, or temptation. It is not a sin to be harassed. Jesus was tempted by Satan himself but did not sin.)

2. **Torment** (This is a more serious attack and includes anxiety, panic, fears, severe insomnia, nightmares, and mental anguish. Through no fault of their own, adults and even children can be tormented.)

3. **Possession** (In this least common form of attack, there is a temporary overtaking of the body or tongue by a demonic spirit. We have often been told that a child of God can't have a demon, but that is not true. It was almost exclusively God's people, not pagans, that Jesus set free from demons.)

The Path to Freedom

We can find freedom from the grip of the kingdom of darkness through two powerful responses: *repenting and renouncing.*

1. We *repent* when we come to God with a sorrowful heart and ask him for forgiveness.

The sacrifice you desire is a broken spirit. You will not reject a
broken and repentant heart, O God.
Psalm 51:17

But if we confess our sins to him, he is faithful and just to forgive
us our sins and to cleanse us from all wickedness.
1 John 1:9

2. We *renounce* by taking up the authority Jesus gave us to command the enemy to leave us and our loved ones.

So humble yourselves before God.
Resist the devil, and he will flee from you.
James 4:7

A Prayer to Renounce Ancestral Sins

Father, I come before you now asking forgiveness for every way that my parents, grandparents and great grandparents made choices that dishonored you. I renounce and break agreement with their choice to be involved in _____, as well as any unknown sins, and reject those choices now. Please forgive our family and set us free from every attachment and bondage that was formed due to their choices.

In Jesus' name, Amen.

A Prayer of Personal Repentance and Renunciation

God, I admit that I have dishonored and resisted you in many ways. I have rebelled against you. I see now that I was wrong. You are God and I am not! I regret my sinful choices and I ask now for your forgiveness and mercy.

Thank you, God, for giving me the authority to use the name of Jesus to evict every enemy of the cross. I do so now. I renounce every way that I have ever honored the enemy or dishonored my Lord. In the name of Jesus, I hereby reject and evict every scheme of darkness over my life and over the lives of my children. I choose now to worship and serve God alone.

In Jesus' name, Amen.

DISCUSSION QUESTIONS:

1. For which scheme of the enemy have you been more likely to fall—ignorance (doubting the reality of the demonic) or intimidation (living in fear of the demonic)?

2. Satan's forces can find access into our lives through our own sinful choices, the sinful choices of others, or through generational patterns. Which of these doors do you believe could be open in your life?

3. How will you close these doors?

4. Do you see any evidence of a stronghold in your current or past life?

9.1 Soul Ties

People have influence over us, and some have more power to influence us than others. I treasure the positive, godly friendships I've had over the years, especially the one I've had with Susan Moore of Lake City, Florida. When Susan left this life on May 22, 2013 for her home in heaven, she left a lasting imprint on many souls, including my own. Susan was my mentor. There was no formal discussion or agreement. We simply connected at a deep level for well over 30 years. We'd go for months without contact, but could go deep in our conversations or simply sit in moments of quiet when we did reconnect. The invisible connection between us was real and strong—an example of a godly soul tie.

Maybe you've been blessed by a deep connection with another person based on a healthy exchange of love and caring over time. If so, rejoice and treasure that connection! But there are also intense relationships built on a not-so-godly foundation. Relationships based on ungodly ties (like an immoral sexual relationship between two people or the manipulation of one person by another) keep us open to the influence of darkness. We all need to take time to examine our lives for any ungodly relationships and then ask God to sever the ties or connections established by them.

What is a Soul Tie?

A soul tie is defined as an open connection between the souls of two people. Soul ties can be godly or ungodly, depending on their nature. One common example of a godly soul tie would be a marriage of two believers:

> *"Haven't you read the Scriptures?" Jesus replied.*
> *"They record that from the beginning 'God made them male and*
> *female.'" And He said, "This explains why a man leaves*
> *his father and mother and is joined to his wife, and the two are*
> *united into one. Since they are no longer two but one, let no one*
> *split apart what God has joined together."*
> Matthew 19:4-6

Also, like my relationship with Susan, godly soul ties can also be established when two people share a friendship with God's love connecting them. This was true of the close relationship between the future King David and Prince Jonathan:

> *So Jonathan made a solemn pact with David, saying,*
> *"May the Lord destroy all your enemies!" And Jonathan made*
> *David reaffirm his vow of friendship again, for Jonathan*
> *loved David as he loved himself...*
> 1 Samuel 20:16-17

Ungodly Soul Ties

What then is an ungodly soul tie? One example is a sexual relationship with someone other than our own spouse.

And don't you realize that if a man joins himself to a prostitute,
he becomes one body with her? For the Scriptures say,
"The two are united into one."
1 Corinthians 6:16

God designed two to become one in the expression of marital sexuality. Sexual oneness creates an open channel between the two people involved. Spirits of darkness can pass from one to the other through the open connection.

We are wise to ask God to sever any open links that were created even years ago between us and those with whom we have had past sexual relationships.

Unfortunately, the enemy of our souls fights dirty. Spirits of lust or perversion often attach to innocent children or adults due to child sexual abuse or rape. It is common to see repeat victimization of those who've been taken advantage of in the past. Why? It's as if the spirit of lust that resided in the perpetrator now calls out from the innocent victim to future perpetrators, "Over here—this one's been conditioned not to fight."

Another example of an ungodly soul tie is a manipulative or controlling relationship between any two people. Queen Jezebel of Israel was known for a spirit of manipulation coming from witchcraft. She controlled her husband Kind Ahab for years:

No one else so completely sold himself to what was evil in the
Lord's sight as Ahab did under the influence of his wife Jezebel.
His worst outrage was worshiping idols just as the Amorites had
done—the people whom the Lord had driven out from the land
ahead of the Israelites.
1 Kings 21:25

Pursuing Freedom

By activating our wills, not our emotions, we can ask for forgiveness and invite the Spirit of God to sever any ungodly soul tie we have chosen. Beginning with sexual soul ties, list any previous relationships you have had that involved sexual activity outside of marriage (or in previous marriages):

_____

_____

_____

_____

Now pray this prayer over each and every person with whom you were involved:

Prayer of Release from Sexual Soul Ties

Heavenly Father, in the name of the Lord Jesus Christ, and as an act of my free will, I confess and renounce my involvement in the sin of sexual immorality. I ask you to sever any soul tie that may have been established because of my relationship with _____.
I ask that you send back to _____ any part of him/her that was left with me and that you bring back to me any part of myself that was left with them.
Father, I ask you to forgive me. I now choose to forgive myself and I release myself from any guilt or shame concerning this area of sin. In the name of the Lord Jesus Christ, I cancel all of Satan's power and authority over me because of the sin of sexual immorality and/or the soul tie with _____, because God has forgiven me and I have forgiven myself. It is finished.
In the name of Jesus, Amen.

Soul Ties Resulting from Unwanted Sexual Contact

List any previous relationships you have had that involved *unwanted* sexual contact:

_____

_____

_____

Prayer of Release from Unwanted Sexual Soul Ties

Heavenly Father, in the name of the Lord Jesus Christ and as an act of my free will, I ask you to sever any ungodly soul tie that may have been established because of my relationship with _____. I ask that you send back to _____ any part of him/herself that was left with me and bring back to me any part of myself that was left with them.
Father, I now choose to forgive my offender. I proclaim my innocence and release myself from any guilt or shame concerning this area. In the name of the Lord Jesus Christ, I cancel all of Satan's power and authority over me from being drawn into the sin of sexual immorality. It is finished.
In the name of Jesus Christ, Amen.

Control/Manipulation Soul Ties

List any relationships you now have or have had that involved control and/or manipulation:

_____
_____
_____
_____

Prayer of Release from Control/Manipulation Soul Ties

Heavenly Father, in the name of the Lord Jesus Christ and as an act of my free will, I confess that I have allowed myself to be manipulated or controlled by _____. I ask you to sever any ungodly soul tie that may have been established because of my relationship with them. I ask that you send back to _____ any part of him/herself that was left with me and bring back to me any part of myself that was left with them.

Father, I choose now to forgive _____ for using me wrongfully. I ask you to forgive me for any way this relationship dishonored you. I now choose to forgive myself and I release myself from any guilt or shame concerning this area. In the name of the Lord Jesus Christ, I cancel all of Satan's power and authority over me because God has forgiven me and I have forgiven myself.
It is finished.
In the name of Jesus Christ, Amen.

DISCUSSION QUESTIONS:

1. As a group, discuss the difference between godly and ungodly soul ties. Individually, list any godly soul ties (think of marriages, mentors, and close friendships) you have had:

2. Have you noticed that some people are able to get you to do what they want you to do, almost against your will? Could this be evidence of an ungodly soul tie? List them here:

3. Has your life been negatively affected by anyone with whom you've been linked sexually?

4. List all past and current voluntarily chosen ungodly sexual relationships:

5. List all past and current unwanted ungodly sexual relationships:

9.2 God Times

The Lord hears His people when they call to Him for help. He rescues them from all their troubles. The Lord is close to the brokenhearted; He rescues those whose spirits are crushed.
Psalms 34:17-18

Have you ever missed someone so badly you felt physically ill? When I was 19 and he was 24, I married Ray Callahan. Ray had learned to love flying as an air crewman in the Navy. In the early months of our marriage, he began flight training to become a pilot himself. About two months after our wedding, Ray had to make a five-day cross-country trip from our home in Riverside, California to Farmington, New Mexico. It was only 5 days. But the year was 1971 and there were no cell phones or email. We couldn't even afford a long distance call on our budget. I kept telling myself I needed to be mature but I spent a miserable five days, waiting impatiently for Ray's return.

Have you ever felt that way? Have you had an intense longing to be with someone special? What exactly was it that motivated you to do whatever you could to be with that person? Can you and I experience that same sense of connection in our relationship with God?

The depth of desire is determined by the depth of connection between two beings. This kind of connection or communion can be defined as the sharing or exchanging of intimate thoughts and feelings, especially when the exchange is on a mental or spiritual level. Communion is a connection between two people that gives life and joy. It is definitely *not* a duty or an obligation. No one had to force me to want to spend time with my new husband. Think about that as we consider what it means to have a 'God Time.'

If you grew up in a church setting, you may have heard the habit of spending time with God called 'devotions' or a 'quiet time.' We've probably all been convinced that this is something good, but it's just as likely that few of us have experienced *consistent* God Times. Before going further, let's make clear what God Times are and what they are not:

What Good God Times are:

- Growth-inducing
- Stress-relieving
- Life-changing
- Healing to body, soul and spirit

What Good God Times are not:

- Legalistic (compulsory, performance-based, guilt-inducing)
- Dry
- Boring
- A Burden

Scripture tells us that Jesus regularly enjoyed time with his heavenly Father. In fact, he made it a priority:

But the news about Jesus spread even more. So crowds of people came to hear Him.

> *They also came to be healed of their sicknesses. But Jesus often*
> *went away to be by Himself and pray.*
> Luke 5:15-17

Spending time with God was also a priority as well as a joy for the writers of the book of Psalms:

> *A single day in your courts is better than a thousand anywhere*
> *else! I would rather be a gatekeeper in the house of my God than*
> *live the good life in the homes of the wicked.*
> Psalm 84:10

> *As a deer longs for streams of water, so I long for you, O God.*
> *I thirst for God, the living God.*
> Psalm 42:1-2

If it's such a good thing, why are so few of us taking advantage of time with God? Part of the answer may lie in the fact that human beings don't always recognize two important things about the spiritual side of their nature:

- We were created with a need for God. People wander from one hobby or interest to the next, chasing fulfillment but never quite finding it.

- God alone holds the key to fulfillment of the 'spirit being' inside each of us.

God's Promise

Should we decide to pursue time with our Creator, we will find some encouragement waiting for us. God promises that if we seek Him we *will* find Him!

> *But from there you will search again for the LORD your God.*
> *And if you search for Him with all your heart and soul,*
> *you will find Him.*
> Deuteronomy 4:29

King David experienced an unusual depth of intimacy with God. He brought his pain and frustration as well as his joy and worship before God daily. Read through the Psalms for yourself to see the breadth and depth of that relationship. Before transferring the throne to his son, David gave Solomon his best advice:

> *And Solomon, my son, learn to know the God of your ancestors*
> *intimately. Worship and serve Him with your whole heart and a*
> *willing mind. For the Lord sees every heart and knows every plan*
> *and thought. If you seek Him, you will find Him. But if you forsake*
> *Him, He will reject you forever.*
> 1 Chronicles 28:9

Three Motivations for Having a Regular God Time

1. The Motivation of Desperation or Pain

Because of our own wrong choices or because of the choices of others, life often brings us to a place of true desperation or pain. No one wants it but few of us are able to avoid it. You may call it a 'foxhole prayer,' but this kind of deep pain causes us to cry out to God almost involuntarily.

The waves of death overwhelmed me; floods of destruction swept
over me. The grave wrapped its ropes around me; death laid a trap
in my path. But in my distress I cried out to the LORD;
yes, I cried to my God for help. He heard me from
His sanctuary; my cry reached His ears.
2 Samuel 22:5-7

2. The Motivation of Hunger

In David's words to Solomon, "Worship and serve Him with your whole heart and a willing mind." Pursue God. Get hungry for His presence. Once you discover the peace, comfort and wisdom available there, you will want more.

Blessed are those who hunger and thirst for righteousness
for they will be filled.
Matthew 5:6

God will always give what is right to His people who cry to Him
night and day, and He will not be slow to answer them.
Luke 18:7 NCV

It's okay to begin by admitting you are NOT hungry enough to be consistent in your God times. That was my problem. I knew I *should* have a regular God time, but somehow it never became a part of my daily life. A few years ago, I realized I was going to have to outsmart myself if I was ever going to develop this habit. I knew that there were one or two things without which I would be unwilling to start my day. One was eating breakfast. I chose to refuse to eat anything until I'd had my God time. I did this for a period of one year and it worked! I developed a strong hunger for time with God, soon extending the time I allowed from 15 minutes to 45 minutes. If you want to try this but don't care about eating breakfast, try refusing to get dressed until you've had your God time. God will honor your desire to *become* hungry!

3. The Motivation of Need

A baby cries for its mother because it knows instinctively that it needs her and could die without her help and attention. But we can easily slip into a self-reliant mode as adults, convincing ourselves that we're fine, that we don't need God or anyone else. God will allow us to travel through life's path alone, but He also allows us to suffer from spiritual deprivation in order to draw us to him. It's all a matter of humbling ourselves and recognizing our need:

Blessed are those who recognize they are spiritually helpless.
The kingdom of heaven belongs to them.
Matthew 5:3 GW

The Lord is good to those who depend on Him,
to those who search for Him.
Lamentations 3:25

In his book *The Power of Crying Out*, Bill Gothard explains the difference between simply praying and *crying out* to God. The Hebrew word meaning 'to cry out' is *ze'akah*. There are many *ze'akah* verses, all indicating that crying out draws God's special attention to our situation. Here are just a few:

But in my distress I cried out to the Lord;
yes, I cried to my God for help.
He heard me from His sanctuary; my cry reached His ears.
2 Samuel 22:7

I cry out to the Lord; I plead for the Lord's mercy. I pour out my
complaints before Him and tell Him all my troubles. When I am
overwhelmed, You alone know the way I should turn.
Psalm 142:1-3

Righteous people cry out. The Lord hears and rescues them from all
their troubles. The Lord is near to those whose hearts are humble.
He saves those whose spirits are crushed.
Psalm 34:17-18 (GW)

How Do I Connect With God?

If you've never had a regular God time, you might want to try what Pastor David Saathoff calls the 13 Minute Plan:

- 5 minutes of Bible-reading
- 5 minutes of prayer
- 3 minutes of mediation and/or journaling

Other elements you might include are: listening to worship music, reading a devotional book, practicing listening prayer, and memorizing scripture. Also take in a good book on the spiritual disciplines like Richard Foster's *Celebration of Discipline* or John Ortberg's *The Life You've Always Wanted*.

Is There a Best Time?

- A set time on a daily basis creates a good habit: morning, noon, or evening
- An entire day once every month or two deepens your connection with God even more
- A whole weekend once a year is a great way to connect with God

Remember His promise to you if you do:

> *This is what the Lord says, He who made the earth,*
> *the Lord who formed it and established it—*
> *the Lord is His name: 'Call to me and I will answer you*
> *and tell you great and unsearchable things you do not know.'*
> Jeremiah 33:2-3

Recommended Devotional Guides:

Jesus Calling by Sarah Young
My Utmost for His Highest: Updated Edition by Oswald Chambers
The Power of Crying Out by Bill Gothard
YouVersion.com (Free Bible reading plans and devotionals)
ivpress.com Free online Daily Devotional

DISCUSSION QUESTIONS:

1. Have you had any experience with regular God times? Describe your experience:

2. Did these times fit more into the legalistic, dry category or would you describe them as life-giving communion? Why?

3. What are some things you could do to help move you from "I should" to "I want to"?

4. What have you discovered that has helped you make these times consistent?

5. What new elements have you tried or would you like to try?

10.0 Service

Principle Ten

**I overcome by choosing a lifestyle that expresses
God's love to a hurting world in practical ways.**

*For you have been called to live in freedom, my brothers and
sisters. But don't use your freedom to satisfy your sinful nature.
Instead, use your freedom to serve one another in love. For the
whole law can be summed up in this one command: "Love your
neighbor as yourself."*
Galatians 5:13-14

Having experienced the grace and healing of God over the past few months, we are now ready to move on to the final principle in our transformation process: becoming more like Christ by giving our lives away in service to others. The New Testament book of Philippians is dedicated to this theme. In the original Greek text, the word *paradidomi* is used to express the concept on which we wish to focus. *Paradidomi* is a compound word literally meaning "over" and "to give." So *paradidomi* means to give your life away:

*Don't be selfish; don't try to impress others. Be humble, thinking
of others as better than yourselves. Don't look out only for your
own interests, but take an interest in others, too. You must have the
same attitude that Christ Jesus had. Though he was God, he did not
think of equality with God as something to cling to.
Instead, he gave up his divine privileges; he took the humble
position of a slave and was born as a human being.
When he appeared in human form, he humbled himself in obedience
to God and died a criminal's death on a cross.*
Philippians 2:3-8

Although he was God, Jesus modeled the life of a servant. He certainly didn't have to. He could have claimed his divine rights as King of heaven and earth and demanded worship and honor. But he chose instead to live a life of loving service, a life that put others first. Jesus lived what he taught. He made sacrifices every day to bring healing and hope to those around him. Then he made the ultimate sacrifice, giving his life for us when we'd done nothing to deserve it.

*We know what real love is because Jesus gave up his life for us.
So we also ought to give up our lives for our brothers and sisters.*
1 John 3:16

Now it's our turn. We have the opportunity to live for ourselves or to give our lives away in service to others. One such story is contained in the book *To End All Wars*, written by WWII British Army officer Ernest Gordon. Gordon tells the story of being captured by the Japanese and sent to work on a railway in the swamps of Thailand. Like 80,000 others, Gordon almost died of malaria, dysentery and typhoid. But as he lay dying, an event took place that changed everything. Here's the story:

The guards had accused the prisoners of stealing a shovel and demanded to know who had taken it. When no one confessed, a guard shouted, "All die! All die!" and raised his rifle to fire on the first man in line. At this instant an enlisted man stepped forward and said, "I did it." The guard fell on him in a fury, beating and kicking him and finally bashing in his skull with the butt of his gun. But that evening when the tools were inventoried a second time, it was discovered that the guards had miscounted. No shovel was missing.

When this fact circulated among the prisoners, one of them remembered the verse that says, *"No greater love hath any man than to lay down his life for his friends."* With that example to follow the attitudes in the camp began to change.

Gordon personally benefitted. Some of his friends built a new bamboo addition onto their hut and moved Gordon into it. Two others cared for his wounds. Another brought him food and cleaned his latrine daily. As Gordon recovered, other prisoners who knew he had studied philosophy asked him to lead a discussion group on ethics. This led to the beginning of a 'jungle university' where prisoners with certain expertise taught courses on history, mathematics, economics, and foreign languages. Artists produced enough material to hold an art exhibit. Botanists planted a garden with medicinal herbs. Musicians carved woodwinds out of bamboo and formed an orchestra.

While that jungle camp never became home, it did change drastically. It changed because one enlisted man gave his life away and set an example for others to follow.

Finding Your 'Sweet Spot'

While few of us will be challenged to choose to die for others, all of us can choose to live for the hurting people around us. You may already feel drawn to a particular need in your local community or even globally. Great! God will use you in amazing ways as you step up and set out in faith. If not, take the time now to find your own 'sweet spot' by examining the following three areas of your life: your unique place, your unique people, and your unique passion.

1. Your unique place

What are the needs in your immediate community? Are you in a rural area, the suburbs, or an inner city? Because she knows the children in her school often have no food available to them when they leave campus, one teacher I know gives a large percentage of her salary to feed inner city kids in her school every day from 3-6pm.

2. Your unique people

What kinds of hurting people exist near you? Are there homeless people or teen mothers or single moms barely getting by? Take time to explore the facts and needs.

3. Your unique passion

Ask yourself, "What has God given me a passion to see changed—what has he brought me through or healed me from?" You may feel called to reach out to the addicted. Jump in! Be a sponsor or lead a group. Or maybe like my friend Chuck Paul, Director of the Alamo Youth Center, you have a passion to confront and end human trafficking. Big and small, the needs are almost endless, so discover your passion and then go for it.

*This concept was developed and is further explained by Will Mancini in *Church Unique*.

A Word of Caution...

It's important to understand that living a life of service to others is NOT a way to be made right with God. We become a child of God the moment we place our faith in the sacrifice of Christ to pay our sin debt. God's grace covers us instantly and completely. Well-known reformer of the Christian faith, Martin Luther, struggled with the simplicity of this truth for years:

> "Although I was an impeccable monk, I stood before God as a sinner with a troubled conscience.... Night and day I pondered until I saw the connection between the justice of God and the truth that, "the just shall live by faith." Then I grasped that the justice of God is the righteousness by which God justifies us by faith. When I realized this truth for myself, I felt reborn. I felt like I had gone through open doors into paradise. If you have faith that Christ is your Savior, that faith leads you to experience God's heart of pure grace and overflowing love."
> — Martin Luther

The Christian life *begins* when we receive the gift of eternal life in Christ but it finds *fulfillment* in a life dedicated to following the example and instruction of Christ himself, a life of *paradidomi*.

Living a Paradidomi Life

Jesus said if we want to find real life, we'll stop focusing on selfish desires and choose instead a life dedicated to serving others. One day he openly told his disciples that he was on his way to Jerusalem to suffer, be rejected, and die. Peter reprimanded him for this, but Jesus called all his disciples and the nearby crowd to him and said:

> ***If any of you wants to be my follower, you must turn from your selfish ways, take up your cross, and follow me. If you try to hang on to your life, you will lose it. But if you give up your life for my sake and for the sake of the Good News, you will save it.***
> Mark 8:34-35

It's our choice. We can choose the self-life, one in which all we think about is me, myself and I. But we can also choose to live the *paradidomi* life...

➤ *Paradidomi* is about loving others. (The self-life is about loving me.)

➤ *Paradidomi* is willing to suffering for others. (The self-life is about protecting myself from pain.)

➢ *Paradidomi* is about generously sharing what you have with others. (The self-life is about obtaining and consuming more and more 'stuff.')

We can make the *paradidomi* choice. If we do we're likely to hear these sweet words from our own Lord someday: "Well done, my good and faithful servant. You have been faithful in handling this small amount, so now I will give you many more responsibilities. Let's celebrate together!"

DISCUSSION QUESTIONS:

1. What does it mean to you to live a life of *paradidomi*?

2. Who has impacted your life because of their lifestyle of serving others?

3. Give an example of a time when you made the *paradidomi* choice.

4. Give an example of a time when you made the self-life choice.

5. Have you found your own 'sweet spot'? Describe what you believe are your unique passions, unique people, and unique place:

Appendix A

LIFE INVENTORY

RESENTMENTS LIST/HARMS LIST
(Feel free to make additional copies of each as needed)

RESENTMENTS

WHO List people or groups that you resent or fear	WHAT Briefly state what they did that harmed you	HOW How did this affect you?	MY PART Where were you at fault in your words, thoughts or actions?	ACTION NEEDED Forgive/ Make Amends/ Set Boundaries

RESENTMENTS

WHO	WHAT	HOW	MY PART	ACTION NEEDED
List people or groups that you resent or fear	Briefly state what they did that harmed you	How did this affect you?	Where were you at fault in your words, thoughts or actions?	Forgive/ Make Amends/ Set Boundaries

RESENTMENTS

WHO List people or groups that you resent or fear	WHAT Briefly state what they did that harmed you	HOW How did this affect you?	MY PART Where were you at fault in your words, thoughts or actions?	ACTION NEEDED Forgive/ Make Amends/ Set Boundaries

RESENTMENTS

WHO List people or groups that you resent or fear	WHAT Briefly state what they did that harmed you	HOW How did this affect you?	MY PART Where were you at fault in your words, thoughts or actions?	ACTION NEEDED Forgive/ Make Amends/ Set Boundaries

RESENTMENTS

WHO	WHAT	HOW	MY PART	ACTION NEEDED
List people or groups that you resent or fear	Briefly state what they did that harmed you	How did this affect you?	Where were you at fault in your words, thoughts or actions?	Forgive/ Make Amends/ Set Boundaries

RESENTMENTS

WHO	WHAT	HOW	MY PART	ACTION NEEDED
List people or groups that you resent or fear	Briefly state what they did that harmed you	How did this affect you?	Where were you at fault in your words, thoughts or actions?	Forgive / Make Amends / Set Boundaries

RESENTMENTS

WHO List people or groups that you resent or fear	WHAT Briefly state what they did that harmed you	HOW How did this affect you?	MY PART Where were you at fault in your words, thoughts or actions?	ACTION NEEDED Forgive / Make Amends / Set Boundaries

RESENTMENTS

WHO	WHAT	HOW	MY PART	ACTION NEEDED
List people or groups that you resent or fear	Briefly state what they did that harmed you	How did this affect you?	Where were you at fault in your words, thoughts or actions?	Forgive / Make Amends / Set Boundaries

RESENTMENTS

WHO List people or groups that you resent or fear	WHAT Briefly state what they did that harmed you	HOW How did this affect you?	MY PART Where were you at fault in your words, thoughts or actions?	ACTION NEEDED Forgive/ Make Amends/ Set Boundaries

RESENTMENTS

WHO	WHAT	HOW	MY PART	ACTION NEEDED
List people or groups that you resent or fear	Briefly state what they did that harmed you	How did this affect you?	Where were you at fault in your words, thoughts or actions?	Forgive/ Make Amends/ Set Boundaries

HARMS

WHO List people or groups you've harmed physically, emotionally, verbally, financially, or sexually	WHAT Briefly state what you did or failed to do that caused harm	MY PART (Anger, broken promises, controlling, lying, lust, pride, etc.)	MY BASIC NEEDS Which basic need drove this action?	ACTION NEEDED Forgive / Make Amends / Set Boundaries

HARMS

WHO List people or groups you've harmed physically, emotionally, verbally, financially, or sexually	WHAT Briefly state what you did or failed to do that caused harm	MY PART (Anger, broken promises, controlling, lying, lust, pride, etc.)	MY BASIC NEEDS Which basic need drove this action?	ACTION NEEDED Forgive/ Make Amends/ Set Boundaries

HARMS

WHO List people or groups you've harmed physically, emotionally, verbally, financially, or sexually	WHAT Briefly state what you did or failed to do that caused harm	MY PART (Anger, broken promises, controlling, lying, lust, pride, etc.)	MY BASIC NEEDS Which basic need drove this action?	ACTION NEEDED Forgive/ Make Amends/ Set Boundaries

HARMS

WHO List people or groups you've harmed physically, emotionally, verbally, financially, or sexually	WHAT Briefly state what you did or failed to do that caused harm	MY PART (Anger, broken promises, controlling, lying, lust, pride, etc.)	MY BASIC NEEDS Which basic need drove this action?	ACTION NEEDED Forgive/ Make Amends/ Set Boundaries

HARMS

WHO List people or groups you've harmed physically, emotionally, verbally, financially, or sexually	WHAT Briefly state what you did or failed to do that caused harm	MY PART (Anger, broken promises, controlling, lying, lust, pride, etc.)	MY BASIC NEEDS Which basic need drove this action?	ACTION NEEDED Forgive/ Make Amends/ Set Boundaries

HARMS

WHO	WHAT	MY PART	MY BASIC NEEDS	ACTION NEEDED
List people or groups you've harmed physically, emotionally, verbally, financially, or sexually	Briefly state what you did or failed to do that caused harm	(Anger, broken promises, controlling, lying, lust, pride, etc.)	Which basic need drove this action?	Forgive/ Make Amends/ Set Boundaries

HARMS

WHO List people or groups you've harmed physically, emotionally, verbally, financially, or sexually	WHAT Briefly state what you did or failed to do that caused harm	MY PART (Anger, broken promises, controlling, lying, lust, pride, etc.)	MY BASIC NEEDS Which basic need drove this action?	ACTION NEEDED Forgive/ Make Amends/ Set Boundaries

HARMS

WHO List people or groups you've harmed physically, emotionally, verbally, financially, or sexually	WHAT Briefly state what you did or failed to do that caused harm	MY PART (Anger, broken promises, controlling, lying, lust, pride, etc.)	MY BASIC NEEDS Which basic need drove this action?	ACTION NEEDED Forgive/ Make Amends/ Set Boundaries

HARMS

WHO List people or groups you've harmed physically, emotionally, verbally, financially or sexually	WHAT Briefly state what you did or failed to do that caused harm	MY PART (Anger, broken promises, controlling, lying, lust, pride, etc.)	MY BASIC NEEDS Which basic need drove this action?	ACTION NEEDED Forgive / Make Amends / Set Boundaries

HARMS

WHO List people or groups you've harmed physically, emotionally, verbally, financially, or sexually	WHAT Briefly state what you did or failed to do that caused harm	MY PART (Anger, broken promises, controlling, lying, lust, pride, etc.)	MY BASIC NEEDS Which basic need drove this action?	ACTION NEEDED Forgive/ Make Amends/ Set Boundaries

Appendix B

BASIC NEEDS/INSTINCTS

Which of these basic needs or instincts was driving your behavior at the time?

Security Needs/Instincts

Bonding
Emotional stability
Financial stability
Stable home
Job
Material goods
Power (the right to say no)
Safety
Spirituality (connection with God)
Trust
Worth

Social Needs/Instincts

Acceptance
Affirmation
Approval
Affection
Attention
Belonging
Comfort
Encouragement
Forgiveness
Emotional Intimacy
Love
Relationships
Respect
Self-esteem
Support

Sexual Needs/Instincts

Acceptable
God-given
Loving Union
Normal
Physical intimacy
Security

Negative Motivators

Addiction
Codependency/rescuing
Controlling others
Ego
Fear
Feeling Unloved
Greed
Insecurity
Jealousy
Low self-esteem
Lust
Neediness
Perversion
Pride
Rejection
Selfishness
Self-righteousness
Withholding

Appendix C

MY PART

Ask yourself, "Where was I at fault in my words, thoughts or actions?" Here is a partial list meant to prompt your thoughts:

Angry	Negative
Anxious	Perfectionistic
Bitter	Playing God
Broken promises	Poor boundaries
Controlling	Poor decisions
Deceiving	Powering up
Fearful	Prideful
Gluttonous	Procrastinating
Greedy	Resentful
Grief-stricken	Revengeful
Gossipy	Saving face
Guilty	Self-pitying
Guilt-inducing	Selfish
Ignorant	Stealing
Inappropriately touching	Stubborn
Insecure	Tired
Jealous	Unforgiving
Judging	Unloving
Lazy	Unrealistic expectations
Lonely	Using another
Lying	Violent/Harming
Lustful	Withdrawing
Mean	Withholding

Appendix D

CHARACTER FLAWS

Aggressive
Angry
Apathetic
Afraid
Argumentative
Arrogant
Attacking
Avoidant
Boastful
Careless
Cheating
Compulsive
Conceited
Contemptuous
Controlling
Cowardly
Critical
Cynical
Deceitful
Defensive
Denying
Dependent
Depressed
Dishonest
Disloyal
Disobedient
Disrespectful
Enabling
Envying
Exaggerating

Disloyal
Fearful
Forgetful
Gluttonous
Gossiping
Greedy
Hateful
Hypersensitive
Ill-tempered
Impatient
Impulsive
Inconsiderate
Indecisive
Insecure
Intolerant
Irresponsible
Isolated
Jealous
Judgmental
Lazy
Loud
Manipulative
Nagging
Narrow-minded
Obscene, crude
Over-emotional
Perfectionistic
Pessimistic
Possessive
Procrastinating

Rationalizing
Resentful, bitter
Rude
Sarcastic
Self-centered
Self-destructive
Self-hating
Self-justifying
Self-pitying
Self-righteous
Selfish
Shy
Stealing
Stubborn
Sullen
Superior
Superstitious
Tense
Undisciplined
Unfriendly
Ungrateful
Unkind
Unreliable
Vindictive
Violent
Vulgar
Wasteful
Withdrawn
Wordy

Appendix E

TIPS FOR GROUP LEADERS

Congratulations—you are about to embark on an amazing journey! Leading a life transformation group can be incredibly rewarding. Your influence and leadership style is key to the success of the group.

Things to Know:

- Leader requirements: Ideally, leaders should have been through the H2O process themselves. They should be growing believers who are committed to live as examples to members, including making a commitment to sobriety and to sexual purity. It's best to have two leaders for each group. This allows for shared responsibility and continuity in case of illness or emergencies on the part of the leaders and for two role models for the group.

- Length: The H2O Workbook material itself encompasses 21 weeks. Add one week for Orientation at the beginning and a week for Celebration at the end for a total of **23 weeks**. During Orientation you will explain the process, expectations, guidelines, and answer questions. The remainder of the session should allow for individuals to begin sharing. Here are some good opening questions: "Why did you decide to join our group?", "What do you hope to get from the group?", or "If one thing in your life could be different as a result of this group, what would it be?" Close by assigning homework (they should read the Introduction chapter and answer the questions) and praying over the group. You can pray as you feel led or you can lead the group in praying the Serenity Prayer out loud together.

- Time: One and a half to two hours once a week is best.

- Format: Open with prayer, read the Guidelines, and go over the chapter for that week. (You can have members take turns reading it aloud or you can hit the high points of the chapter yourself.) Then ask each member to share the answer they wrote and elaborate as they desire, remembering to limit their comments to 3-5 minutes each time they share. Leaders can get the process going by reading their own responses. End with a leader prayer or have the group recite the Serenity Prayer.

- Expectations: Each member will need to commit to attend faithfully, to read each week's assigned chapter, and to write out and share their answers to the discussion questions. The process works because all members choose to be committed and to share honestly. (It is helpful to have them make this commitment in writing on a form you provide during Orientation.) Gently confront anyone not attending regularly, perhaps suggesting that they sign up for the next group if this is not a good time for them.

- Size & Composition: Ideal group size is 8-10, but it's possible to make the process work with as few as 3 and as many as 12 members, including the leaders. Although you may need to hold a co-ed group as you launch the program, gender-specific groups are best as they encourage deeper levels of sharing.

- Leader Style: Be transparent. Your honesty about your own past struggles will encourage your group to be honest also and not to fear judgment. Be brief. It's important not to overshare or to use this time to process your own issues. Seek counsel with a pastor or other leader if you feel the need. You are worth it!

- The Importance of Guidelines: Maintaining the five guidelines is *essential* to the health and safety of the group. If you don't enforce the guidelines, your group will begin to suffer and may become unsafe. The key is to be kind but firm, avoiding embarrassing members whenever possible. They should be read at the beginning of *every* group.

  1. Members promise to safeguard the confidentiality of everyone in the group, not discussing outside of class anything another group member has revealed (even with one another). Everyone needs a promise of confidentiality in order to encourage honesty in sharing. This is taken so seriously that members should be reassured that anyone who violates confidentiality (after one warning) will be asked privately to leave the group.

  2. Group leaders will keep all comments confidential, with the exception of threatened harm to self or others (we will call 911 if someone threatens to harm themselves or another) or the revelation of abuse of a child (we will call the Child Abuse hotline).

  3. Members will resist the temptation to advise others, focusing instead on their own healing. This includes allowing others to fully experience their emotions without interruption (such as offering them a tissue). It's important not to allow crosstalk. Crosstalk happens when 2 or more individuals hold a conversation, excluding other group members. Group time is reserved for group. Members can stay after group time if they want to share further one on one.

  4. All members agree to restrict their comments to 3-5 minutes in order to allow others equal time to share. You will almost always have members who 'overshare' and some who hesitate to share at all. To keep the group moving, have one leader keep track of time and give a 'time out' signal when members go over their time. Ensure that quiet members are given time to answer every question.

  5. All members agree to avoid the use of profanity. Usually the reading of this guideline is enough to keep members on the right track. It is okay to overlook an occasional slip, but repeat offenders should be gently reminded of the guideline.

Optional Retreat(s):

A retreat is a great way to increase group bonding and increase the impact of the transformation process. There are two places in the process that a retreat would be helpful.

The first is an **Inventory Retreat** to be scheduled just after you complete Principle Three. This retreat provides a boost to the foot-dragging that can happen as individuals face the inventory process. On Friday night you would cover the chapter on Inventory. On Saturday you'd schedule time for group members to find a quiet place to work on the first two columns of the Resentments

List and then after lunch, on the first two columns of the Harms List. You could plan for four 90 minute individual sessions or for 3 two hour ones. The individual sessions will need to be broken up by time for meals and breaks. Group sharing at the end of the day will provide a debriefing time and will allow anyone experiencing overwhelming emotions to be heard and prayed over. End the retreat on Sunday by allowing each member his/her own prayer/healing time. Have them share an area for which they'd like to receive prayer. Then gather the group around them and have them take turns praying as God directs for that person's healing for specific areas of need.

The second possibility is a **Healing Retreat** scheduled towards the end of the process, perhaps after the chapter on Soul Ties or God Times. You can use Friday night to show the group how to draw a Life Map. Ask them to chart the major events of their lives, putting their life highs and lows on a graph. Before they begin, each leader can share their own life story as an example. Then allow about an hour free time for members to make their own graph, providing poster-sized paper and markers. Let them know they'll be sharing their own story with the group on Saturday. Each member should receive about 40-50 minutes of group time, allowing them 20 minutes to share and 20-30 minutes for the group to pray over and then affirm them. Have the group pray as God directs for healing for specific areas of need. End each individual's time by allowing the members to speak words of affirmation over them (for example: "I see in you a caring heart and an amazing ability to encourage others"). Assign the duty of 'scribe' to one member so that the affirming comments can be written down and given to the person at the end of the session. This can be the most powerful part of the entire process, as God delights to show up and use us to minister to each other. Sunday morning is then reserved for a time of group worship and celebration.

Made in the USA
San Bernardino, CA
12 May 2017